BIG

how to live bigger than you've ever imagined

JEROD M SMITH

Cover design and interior layout by Steven Jeffrey.

To learn more about the ministry of Jerod Smith or Advocates for Africa, visit www.advocatesforafrica.org.

Smith, Jerod.
Big: how to live bigger than you've ever imagined/ Jerod Smith
ISBN-13 978-1503031517
1. Christian life. 2. Christianity. 3 . Self-realization

Printed in the United States of America by CreateSpace.
2014 - First Edition

10 9 8 7 6 5 4 3 2 1

Dedication

To my Savior: Without you, Jesus, I am nothing. Thank you for rescuing me in every way.

To my wife, Katina: Without you believing in me, this book would never have been written. You are the love of my life and my best friend, thank you for following me all over the world. To Grandma Jo: Thank you for showing me what true godly grace looks like.

To the rest of my family: Thank you for putting up with me over the years.

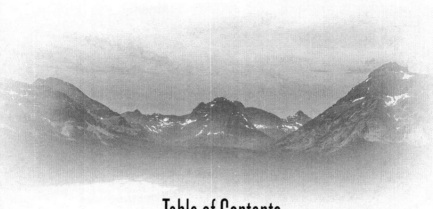

Table of Contents

About the Author

Jerod Smith is a graduate of Victory Bible College and Oklahoma Wesleyan University. He serves as CEO and Founder of the Rwanda based ministry, *Advocates For Africa.* A one-time drug dealer, delivered by the grace of Jesus, Jerod now travels the world speaking of the depth of God's love and forgiveness. He carries an extraordinary desire to see the world, especially the people of Africa, come to know Christ. Remote villages in Africa and large churches in America have been encouraged by his passionate delivery of God's Word.

Jerod and his wife, Katina, live in Kigali, Rwanda where they are working to bring hope, compassion, and education, to the continent of Africa.

Introduction

If we were honest with ourselves, we all would admit that there just seems to be certain things in life that drain our faith quicker than anything else. Financial troubles, sickness, death of a loved one, and even our jagged past, are just a few things that shoot holes in our attempt to believe that God wants the best for us.

When we are drained in our faith, we fall prey to thoughts that God has abandon us. "Where are you God?" We've all made this statement at times. We look at the outside circumstances wreaking havoc in our lives, and wonder why God has not stepped in. While, I don't claim to understand all the workings of God, I do know that He wants the best for

His children. Believing this is where true change begins.

What if I told you that there was a way for you to not only keep your faith through such challenging circumstances, but actually come out stronger in the end? Would you be interested? Of course you would! I believe that by tackling a few key areas which drain your faith, you can become a more passionate and productive believer in Christ. Not only that, but by applying the principles in this book, you will recognize the enormity of God and his great desire for you to trust Him, and begin to believe Him for all things!

So, don't read this book haphazardly, but instead study it. Look up the scriptures references for yourself. Write down the thoughts that the Holy Spirit gives you. Pray for direction, comfort, and renewed passion each day before you read. If you do, soon you'll begin to plug the holes in your spiritual life where faith is draining. You'll feel the refreshing wind of the Holy Spirit. You'll begin to live out the plan that a great BIG God has designed for you!

How BIG is God? Turn the page and let's find out!

Chapter One: God Is Bigger Than Your Problem

It was 3 a.m. when I sat in the hallway of our big house in Butte, Montana with a .45 caliber pistol in the roof of my mouth. Tears rolling down my face and having come to the end of myself, I was fully prepared to end my own life. My wife had taken our son and left for Oklahoma and did not plan to return. I responded to the news by locking myself in the house and going on a three day drinking binge. As I sat there in a train wreck of emotions, retracing the last few years, I could not help but wonder how we had come to this place and time.

The Drive for Success

Our house was located just a block away from the country club and came complete with 36 inches of snow in the front yard all winter. It was much larger than what our family needed, but it served well to portray the image that we wanted everyone around us to see. On the outside we were young professionals that had it all together. We drove nice cars, lived in a big house, made more money than our parents and seemed to have it all. We worked hard to appear successful and in many ways we were.

My drive to be successful was birthed out of a desire to live a different life than what I had as a child. I am a product of a broken home. My parents divorced when I was just a baby, in fact, I never remember them being together. Soon after the divorce both my mother and father remarried. My mother married a man who owned the local bar, and my father married the daughter of an oil tycoon.

The man who became my stepfather ruled his house with an iron fist. Having been raised himself in a household where strict, harsh discipline was the rule; he was quick to dish the same out for my brothers and me. The smallest infraction resulted in incredible punishment. It was an impossible environment, because no matter how hard we tried, there was always some sort of fault that would bring down the punishment.

One of the chores that my little brother and I were assigned was to pick the trash up out of our two-acre yard. We got off the bus and hurried home in an attempt to have it done before he got home for his afternoon break. We walked the yard like investigators looking for clues on a crime scene. Pass after pass, we looked hard for even the smallest evidence that a piece of trash had made its way onto our lawn. After being sure that we had done our best, we returned to the house and waited anxiously.

We watched as his truck came down the road and pulled into our driveway. Many days he got out of his truck and immediately walked into the yard to see if we had done a good job on the trash pick up. Many times my brother and I watched in horror as he would find the smallest piece of trash. Sometimes it would be as small as one shriveled up straw wrapper. He would come into the house and berate us about paying attention to detail, and how we were lazy and could not be trusted with the simplest of tasks. Then down the hall we went for the physical reminder that he was the ruler of the house.

Things were not much better when I went to visit my father on the weekends. His new family seemed to have it all together. They lived in a nice house and went to their lake house for vacation often. The new marriage brought a new stepbrother into my life. At first, I looked up to him. We spent the summer riding the ATVs, going horseback riding and fishing together. He even allowed me to sleep in his room. My naiveté was soon realized when my stepbrother's friendliness turned sexual. Looking back I realize that he was grooming me for what would become years of sexual abuse.

Big In My Own Eyes

When I reached 8th grade, my mom and stepfather had moved to Seattle, Washington, and my father was divorced. This brought an end to the abuse that I was suffering as a child, but it didn't remove the scars that were inflicted. My mother allowed me live with my grandparents after they moved to Seattle, but I was an angry teenager. The years of abuse had brought out the worst in me and those around me suffered the consequences. I can recall many of times that I would bully those around me in an ill attempt to regain my self worth.

As it happens with teenagers who come from situations like mine, I soon began to gain friendships with kids that were partying. At first we just got together to drink. Soon that led us to trying other things. At first we all smoked marijuana, but as I found out, if you run around with people who smoke marijuana there will be a few that do harder drugs. Within a matter of months I found myself doing LSD, and addicted to Crystal Meth. It was the Meth that began to pull me deeper inside the hole that my life had become. It was an expensive habit that I couldn't afford so I started selling a little here and there to make money. This was more addictive than the drugs by a long shot.

I quickly realized the amount of money that could be made in the drug trade, so I went at it as hard as I could. It didn't take long until a friend and I were one of the largest dealers in our county. I was 18 years old and carrying $1500 cash with me at all times. Dealing drugs was dangerous, but I was good at it. I had the clean-cut, innocent look that could help me fly under the radar with ease. People around me did not have a clue how deep into this I really was. Cash, guns, cars, girls, parties, fights; this was my life and I enjoyed the adrenalin that it produced in me, and the fear it produced in others.

Things started to escalate when I began to make contacts that could deal in larger quantities at a much cheaper price. I remember traveling to Dallas once to meet a man about expanding the business across the state line. He had heard through a friend that I could move large amounts of various products in a relatively short amount of time. He spoke to me about his ties to the South American and Mexican cartels. They were looking for guys like me to "mule" their shipments across state lines. It was going to be simple. Pick up a car in the Dallas area, drop it off somewhere in Oklahoma, and make thousands of dollars each month doing so. Not to mention, being able to purchase high quality product at a discounted rate for myself.

It seemed like a perfect set up for someone like me; only something happened that changed my perspective dramatically. I had met a girl that I actually liked spending time with. She was blonde, beautiful and seemed to like me regardless of the money and drugs. She didn't hassle me about my business, but did make it obvious that she was not attracted to me because of those things. It was shocking to me that someone would actually love me for *who* I was, and not *what* I was. We began to grow closer and I soon realized that I wanted to marry her. It was during that trip to Texas to meet my new contact, that I realized that this was no life for her. So I had to make a decision. Do I continue in this business or do I make a change and marry this girl?

The Big Escape

My newly found love combined with the anxiety of dealing with a higher level drug business associate, drove me to realize that I needed to escape this lifestyle. It is not easy to escape a life like I was living because people know you and know where you live. I was not in fear for my life, but rather knowing I could make some serious cash in a short amount of time. It was very difficult to turn people away who wanted to make a large buy. Especially when I soon began to need the money. A larger change was needed than just quitting the drug trade. I needed to leave the area and make a new start. So, I asked Katina to marry me and I enlisted in the Army.

The Army was a good change and a good life for us. We were married in the fall of 1994 and moved into a small two room apartment in Augusta, Georgia. It was not the best neighborhood; in fact the homeless would get drunk and knock on our door to ask for money. That small apartment did more good for us than we realized at the time. Not having a dishwasher, nor a washer and dryer, forced us to spend time together. I remember spending every night washing dishes together. Katina washed and I dried. On the weekends we took our dirty clothes to the Laundromat. I can still recall the hours we spent there, laughing, talking and dreaming of what our lives would be like when we grew old. Those early years of barely getting by financially helped us to bond and grow to love one another in a special way.

In the summer of 1996, my son was born while we were stationed at Ft. Bragg, North Carolina. While I was enjoying the Army and even considering making it a career, having a child brought a whole new set of priorities for me. If you're a parent, you understand when I say that everything I ever wanted instantly became whatever he needed. I began to wonder what kind of life I would be able to provide for my son if I were deployed or worse. The thought of my son growing up with his father gone or dead, didn't appeal to me whatsoever. As I toiled this over in my mind for the next two years, I finally felt that it was best that we leave the Army and enter the civilian workforce.

The Big Crash

My family and I left the Army in 1998 and moved back to my home state of Oklahoma. Most of the people I had associated with in the drug business were incarcerated, dead, or moved away; not to mention that I was a completely different person now. Four years in the Army had helped me to grow up and become the kind of man that I always wanted to be.

I worked in the telecommunications industry, which in the late 90s was booming. We lived in the country and I worked in Tulsa for a great company. I found civilian life to be rather boring so I didn't settle well. Soldiers carry a high level of loyalty to one another and to their mission, whereas most of the civilians I met seemed to be about themselves and the money. This didn't sit well with me so I moved around from company to company for a while.

It wasn't long before I started to get calls from companies out of state to work for them. It was not that I had some special talent, but rather had been on the ground floor with a few companies that became very successful. I had the experience they were looking for, combined with the fact that the industry as a whole was short on experienced people. Knowing this, many in my field would leave their names with corporate recruiters on a continual basis. This produced a variety of offers for us and it was relatively flattering to have companies coming after you.

One such company was in Butte, Montana. They were just launching their fiber network and wanted to hire me as a consultant. I had not previously considered moving that far away from Oklahoma, but when they offered to double my current salary, I was interested. Katina and I talked it over and decided that making that much money combined with the experience that it would give me, would be a good move for us. So we packed our belongings into a moving truck and headed for Butte.

Our first impression of Butte was that it was a cold, drab-looking mining town. There seemed to be mining pits dug all over the landscape, which took away from what would have been mountainous and beautiful. I remember thinking that if someone were looking to move away from it all, that this was certainly the right place. There were very few places to shop but a plethora of local bars to drink in. I'm not sure I've ever been to a place with so many bars. We found a house which we rented sight unseen from the Internet, Katina found a job with a local dentist, and we began to settle into our new life.

The new company was actually further along than what I figured, but there was still lots of work to do in order for them to start turning a profit. Most of the equipment they were using was unfamiliar to the technicians, so I immediately started training them how to troubleshoot the systems. I dove into the work in an attempt to prove that I was the best hire the company had made. Not to mention, they were paying by the hour. I worked from early in the morning until late into the evening trying to get the company settled, but what I didn't realize was the toll this schedule was taking on my home life.

For months I would wake up before my family was awake, and not return until they were in bed for the night. Masked in a cloak of "being a good provider" I relentlessly pursued the money I was making. It was not long until the same high I experienced back in the drug dealing days, was right back with me. I loved the feeling of working hard and being compensated beyond my wildest imagination. I felt that I was providing for my family in a way that I had never been able to do before. We had more money than we honestly knew what to do with.

As you can imagine, a marriage cannot withstand a schedule like this for very long. While, we had everything money could buy, we did not have the love that we once had for one another. My long hours combined with lengthy arguments when I was home drove a wedge into my marriage that I could not see happening. Katina finally decided that she had had enough. She packed up our son, and headed for Oklahoma. What began as just a short-term break quickly turned into a separation. I'll never forget the call I received one afternoon. "I'm not coming back to Butte," my wife said. She went on to explain that she did not want to be married to a man who loved money more than his family. While she was appreciative of me providing for the family, she'd come to the end of her patience with my work schedule and me.

Which brings me back to the hallway after a three day drinking binge. My world had shattered and was falling apart – I never dreamed that I would lose my family in my selfishness to become wealthy. Somewhere it had stopped being about providing and started being about getting more. My best friend in the world – the one I had traveled with, laughed with, and who I loved with all my heart, was now over a thousand miles away and not returning anytime soon. I was broken beyond anything I had ever experienced in my life.

Sitting there in the hallway, a flood of past mistakes raced through my mind. Abuses as a child, drugs, fights, people I had hurt, families I had destroyed, and now the loss of my wife and son. It was too much for me to handle and the enemy of my soul was right there to convince me that the best route was to kill myself. It's interesting how Satan will sit back and wait for the most opportune time to destroy your life. He began to whisper to me, "You've lost it all; you're a failure; God's mad at you; your family hates you; you'll never recover from this." The worst part was that I believed what I was hearing. The pain was unbearable and I wanted it to stop at all costs.

Fully convinced that I had wrecked my life and that God could never forgive me, I placed the gun into the roof of my mouth and began to apply pressure to the trigger. Just at the moment that I was ready to end my life, something powerful began to happen. I suddenly felt a warmth and peace that I had never experienced before. Tears began to roll down my face, as I felt the Spirit of God descend in that hallway. I heard God speak to me words that would forever change my life.

"Where have you been," the Lord said.

I knew in an instant that God had been chasing me my entire life. At every turn, He had tried to reach out to me but I had ignored Him. This time, He simply decided to make me hear Him beyond any doubt.

I placed the gun on the floor and began to repent and weep uncontrollably. Years of pain and sinful living began to pour out of me as I was reawakened to a relationship with God. He reminded me that no hole was too deep, nor place too dark, that He could not bring me out of it. I spent the rest of the night on the floor repenting and crying out to God in a way which would forever impact my future.

As the sun was coming up the next morning, I began the long drive from Montana to Oklahoma. I had to find my wife and at least make an attempt to repair the damage I had done. I made the 20-hour drive quickly only stopping for gas and arrived in Sapulpa, Oklahoma, late in the afternoon. I would love to be able to tell you that I found Katina and we embraced like long lost friends, but that simply wasn't the case. In fact, over the next few days things were rough. We got into a few heated arguments, which left us saying the dreaded word we vowed never to speak in our marriage – *divorce*. I decided to leave it in God's hands because it was obvious that I could never fix the problem in my own power.

After a few days, Katina called me and asked me to meet her at a local park to talk things out. We sat on the back of my Jeep weeping and hurting like you cannot even imagine. We couldn't believe how broken we had allowed our marriage to become. Through a stream of tears we apologized to one another for various wrongs we had committed.

Then, she said something to me that would change the way I viewed God for the rest of my life. Tears and mascara running down her cheeks, she said, "I think all of this has happened to us because we don't have Jesus in our lives."

I could barely believe what I was hearing! I had not mentioned a single word to her about my encounter with God in Montana! I agreed with her and we decided that we needed to talk to a pastor for help.

It so happened that my grandmother's pastor was just a few miles away from us and was at the church that evening. We walked into the small church and I think he realized when he saw us that we were in a desperate crisis in our marriage. He sat us down and began to speak to us about the love and grace of a God who would allow His Son Jesus to die in our place. He convinced me that God really had forgiven me in that hallway and my past had been erased. We all agreed that we should pray and ask Jesus to repair our marriage and commit our lives to Him, so into the dimly-lit sanctuary we went. The pastor, Katina and I knelt at the altar, joined hands, and he led us in a prayer to surrender our lives to Him.

He is Bigger than Your Problem

I don't know why you chose to read this book. Maybe you're going through a hard time and you're wondering if God can help. I'll tell you that for God to become big in your life, you have to begin believing that He loves you enough to help you in your problems. This precept is the foundation of this book and a relationship with God. He is not a God who has forgotten His children, nor does He want them to go through life in pain and misery. In fact, God loves you in a way that is not humanly possible to describe. In order to experience all the fullness of that love you must release your problems to Him. I did, and today my relationship with my stepfather has been restored, I have been married for 20 years and have faithfully served God for many years. The same can happen for you.

Consider what Jesus tells us in Matthew 11:28, 29:

> *Come to Me, all you who labor and are heavy laden, and I will give you rest. Take My yoke upon you and learn from Me, for I am gentle and lowly in heart, and you will find rest for your souls.*

Have you considered why Jesus would tell us to come to him when we are heavy laden? Could it be that He really does love us and want to give us rest from the things that burden us down? Of course He does!

Let's Take This Journey Together

I invite you to keep reading. And consider what God's Word says in 1 Peter 5:7:

Therefore humble yourselves under the mighty hand of God, that He may exalt you in due time, casting all your care upon Him, for He cares for you.

I believe there are a few specific things that weigh us down and make us weary simply because we have not followed the instructions of this verse. Humble yourself and cast your cares upon Him. Doing those two things will put you into a position to live big because a big God will be living through you.

Chapter Two: How Big Is God Really?

"How BIG Is God?"

It's a question that we have to answer. If we can't answer that question correctly, we'll try to line up the things we face in life against God and feel they are bigger and more imposing than Him. We can think that our problems – sickness, financial conditions, work challenges, marital situations, or problems with our teenagers and kids are bigger than God.

The thing to remember is that whenever you face hardships, difficulties or adversity of any kind, we serve a great, BIG enormous God who is able to do more than you ever ask or think. No matter what problems you're facing right now, no matter what it is, from a hangnail to cancer, God is BIG enough to help you deal with it and overcome it! We serve a BIG, BIG God. Although we may forget that at times, God is always ready to move in our midst and on our behalf in a BIG way.

God is Bigger

The biggest building in the world is in Dubai. It's 2,717 feet high. That's a big building. The tallest mountain in the world is Mt. Everest at 29,035 feet. The tallest man ever recorded in history was just under 9 feet tall at 8 feet, 11 inches. His name was Robert Wadlow. Think about that – 8 feet and 11 inches tall. That's a big man! Imagine a guy that tall playing basketball. With the rim at 10 feet high, and without even jumping, all he'd have to do is raise his arms to cover the basket, or dunk a basketball.

Yet out of all the big things there are in the world, there's one thing that's bigger than all of that. When you stack up to anything in your life, anything or everything in this world against God, God is still bigger!

I think that if you asked the general public if there's anything bigger or greater than God, most people would respond that nothing and no one is greater than God. But think about this question for a moment. Do *you* believe that God is bigger and greater than all? Is there anything bigger than Him? He's BIG.

Think of some of the things that He's done in your life. Think of the relationships that have been restored that looked like only a miracle could fix and God stepped into the picture. What about the times when a financial breakthrough was needed and God stepped in and lifted financial pressure from you. God has taken kids that were caught up in drugs, alcohol, violence, and immorality, the ones who nobody thought would ever turn to God, and restored their lives. Only a BIG God can do that. People have been given reports of terminal illness, and received prayer from a group of people that believed God for a healing. The result was God healing what looked impossible to heal. Only a BIG God can do that.

From the very beginning of everything that's recorded in history, God was clearly communicating a truth that would set the standard for all people and for all time. He's bigger than everything and anybody else. Think about how big God is. Let this get ingrained in your spirit and remain foremost in your beliefs every day of your life. In the midst of every problem that comes against you, let your first thoughts be that God is bigger than anything you'll ever face.

God forbid that losing a job should happen to anybody, but when things that have the capacity to change life so dramatically happens, take heart in knowing God is bigger. A job can help provide for needs, but a job is not your supply – God is. He's the One that supplies all your needs according to His provisional riches in glory.

We have God's word on the matter. We have the revelation that God is bigger than the things we can fear coming into our lives. Genesis 1:1 says, *"In the beginning God created the heavens and the earth."* Do you know anybody that could create the heavens and the earth? It would take a pretty big somebody. Genesis 1:2-3 goes on to say, *"And the earth was formless and empty. Darkness was over the surface of the deep and the Spirit of God was hovering over the waters. And God said, Let there be light. And there was light."* All He had to do was speak. The power of words was on display at the very beginning. Look at the pattern:

> *And God said, Let there be an expanse between the waters, to separate the water from the water. And it was so. Genesis 1:6*

> *And God said, Let the water under the sky be gathered to one place, and let dry ground appear, and it was so. Genesis 1:9*

And God said, Let there be lights in the expanse
of the sky to separate the day from the night, and
let them serve as signs to mark the seasons, and the
days, the years, and let them be lights in expanse
of the sky and give light on the earth. And it was
so. Genesis 1:14

And God said, Let the water teem with living
creatures, and let birds fly above the earth across
the expanse of the sky. So God the great creatures
of the sea, and every living and moving thing
with which…the water teems, according to their
kind, every winged bird according to its kind.
God saw that it was good. Genesis 1:20

So far, everything that God said here in Genesis 1, actually
happened. Verse 24 continues:

And (God) said, Let the land produce living crea-
tures according to their kinds, livestock, creatures
that move along the ground, and wild animals,
each according to its kind. And it was so"

Verse 26 is where humanity comes into the picture. "Then
God said, Let us make man in our image." Notice the plural
usage. In our image. In our likeness.

And let them rule over the fish of the sea, and the birds of the air, over the livestock, over all the earth, over all the creatures that move along the ground. So God created man in His own image. In the image of God He created him, male and female He created them. And He blessed them. And He said to them, Be fruitful, and increase in number, fill the earth and subdue it.

God said that man was to take authority over the earth and over his experiences in the earth. Essentially, the God of all creation said to man, "You're in charge of the earth I've created."

God knelt down and out of the dust of the earth He formed man in His own image. And then through the power of the Holy Spirit, He breathed life into His man, Adam. That which was lifeless and just formed out of the dust of the earth began to sit up, stand, and move around. Imagine being Adam, the very first one created. He was given life and didn't even know what he was. But God authorized His creation to be fruitful, multiply, replenish and take authority in the earth. The same power of words with which He brought substance into being was used to establish ownership under His direction. God gave man His world to live in, experience, and rule.

God created woman in the same fashion. Adam and Eve were in the midst of the garden where everything was beautiful and perfect. In this setting was anything mentioned about sickness, disease or lack? We all know something happened that changed things in the earth. But what I want you to understand is that from the very beginning of time God was showing us that He's bigger. Every time we stack a problem we have in our lives up against God, He's bigger.

How big is a God that could say, "Let there be light," and there was light. How big is a God that could say, "Let there be sky," and there was sky. How big is a God that could say, "Let there be land," and there was land. Can you create land? Can you create sky? Can you create the atmosphere and the universe and the stars? I don't know anybody that could do that. I don't know science that could do that. I don't know anybody that could do that but God. And He did it all by just speaking His Word, and it happened.

How big is a God that could let vegetation be brought about on the earth, and a sun and a moon and living creatures upon the earth, and fish of the sea, just by saying "Let there be," and it happened? How big is a God who could take the dust of the ground and form it into a man and breathe life into him? Only a great, BIG, enormous God that's bigger than all your problems. That's what kind of God could do that.

I don't believe it's by accident that you're reading this book. Consider this – why now? Of all the times in your life, why would you pick up this book and begin reading it now? I believe this big God that I'm writing about is bringing you understanding of Himself. You are reading this book now for a reason. He wants you to know that He's BIG. He wants you to know that He's bigger than everything you're facing in your life, both now and in the future.

- *He's bigger than the people who are rejecting you.*

- *He's bigger than the frustrations you're feeling in your work.*

- *He's bigger than the pains and symptoms you're feeling in your body.*

- *He's bigger than your financial challenges.*

- *He's bigger than your insecurities and how inadequate you feel at times.*

- *He's bigger than all that.*

He's the kind of big that the prophet Jeremiah was talking about when he said, "It's You Who have made the heavens and the earth. By Your great power and by Your outstretched arm, nothing's too hard for You." (Jer. 32:17) Nothing is too hard for God to work out, fix, restore, or change for the better. Nothing is too impossible for God to help you beat down, deal with, and overcome.

I want you to say this out loud: "Nothing's too hard for You, God." Now, say it again. Repeat this to God several times until you start to feel it down deep. Repeat it to yourself all day long, and in the midst of your trying times. "Nothing's too hard for You, God!"

God's the kind of big that when Mary was told that she had the Son of God in her womb, and began wondering how such a thing could be, the angel said, "For nothing is impossible with God." Get your mind around that. "Nothing is impossible with God." Pause for a moment and say it to yourself. Nothing is too difficult for God and nothing is impossible for God. Nothing.

You may feel like *no one* understands or cares about what you're going through. Whatever it is, nothing is too difficult for God and nothing is impossible for God. He not only can do something about your problems, but He cares enough to do something to help you. You may be thinking about a doctor's report that very plainly and clearly says this has gone too far and there's nothing that can be done.

You got the *nothing* part right, but the nothing you

want to focus on is that "There's NOTHING too difficult for God, and NOTHING impossible for God." NO THING!

You might be in a situation where you've been out of work for so long that it seems nothing can change. You've tried everything. You've applied everywhere you can think of and been told you're over qualified, under qualified, too young, too old or any number of things. But nothing is too difficult for God. What has seemed impossible to change, God makes possible.

Whatever it is you've got staring you in the face and whatever it's making you feel like, God is big enough to turn it around. Circumstances may tell you that you've lost and there's nothing God can do about it. But God said there's nothing too difficult for Him and there's nothing impossible with Him. Nothing! Think about what is meant by "nothing?" Nothing is zero, zilch, nada, nothing. Not one thing you can think of right now is bigger than God. Nothing is bigger than God.

Speaking about the rich entering heaven in Luke 19, even Jesus Himself said, "With men this (rich men entering heaven) is impossible, but with God all things are possible." All things are possible with God. Jesus wasn't excluding the rich from heaven, nor saying the rich had to forfeit their riches to enter heaven. He was focusing on how God can touch a heart and change a man or woman to make God the center of their lives instead of money, material things, and fame.

You may currently carry hurts from the past, or hurts that have recently happened. You could have all kinds of baggage to deal with. You could have things in your life that make it hard to face the day. You could be in a season of time where it seems everything is stacked against you. People may have doubted you. You may have doubted yourself. It may be hard to hear anything that's presented to you. But through it all, God wants you to know that He's bigger than what you've thought. He's bigger than you can even imagine. And He wants to take your difficult and impossible situations and bring you out from under the pressure.

Where Does it Start?

At this point you may be asking yourself how all this talk about God being big enough to handle your problems can be applied to your life. Where does it start? Consider this, sometimes people think that becoming a Christian is all about joining a religion, but it's not. Christianity has to do with gaining a relationship with a God Who is big enough to handle every detail of our lives, and real enough to know you on a very personal level.

Some people may think that Christianity is only about getting a pass into heaven. Every person has to choose properly when it comes to determining where they're going to spend eternity, because eternity is a long time to get it wrong. Some people think Christianity is only about becoming a better person and acquiring more things. When you follow what God says, being a Christian should make you a better person. Being blessed allows for having quality material goods in life. But that's not all there is to Christianity.

By giving your life to Jesus, it's going to give you access into heaven. Being a better person is in the path of a Christian. By following the counsel of God, the blessing of the Lord can cause riches to come into a person's life. Those things are all parts of what we gain access to when we step into the kingdom of God. When we begin to step into the kingdom of God, and understand how big God is, we're also granted access to God Himself.

No matter what happens in life, we have access to the Creator of the universe. He cares so much about us that even if it's a paper cut, hang nail, sore throat, stomach ache, need for a gallon of gas, or money for the electric bill, God's BIG enough to care about the smallest matters and details of our lives. It also means He's BIG enough to make a way to deal with the most demanding, even catastrophic problems we could ever face. God is just that big.

This isn't a mediocre life that God is calling you into. Ephesians 3:20 tells us that, "He is able to do exceedingly abundantly above all that we ever ask or think." God is able to do even more than what we're praying for. No matter how big we pray, and no matter how big a miracle we need in our lives, it's nothing compared to what God can do and wants to do for us.

What would happen if right this minute, you were to accept this life that God is inviting you to? He's able to do exceedingly and abundantly above all that you ever ask or think. I assure you that if you were to accept His offer of salvation, this life I'm speaking about would be yours today. You'd be brought into a life where God would begin meeting your needs and helping you overcome the difficulties you face.

Maybe you already have. If we were sitting across a table from one another right now, you might say to me "Jerod, I'm a Christian, but I haven't seen God do anything big."

If that's the case, I would ask you what specifically you've asked Him for. Is it big enough? In your business, is it big enough? Are you asking to just barely get by, or are you asking for something huge? You have access to the greatest and most powerful being in the universe. He's a BIG God, and He loves you. He wants to bless you, and He wants to give you the things that you need. I wonder many times if we step right over the things that God has done for us, because we simply didn't recognize them as God. On the contrary, when we ask God for outrageous things and we see it happen, there leaves no doubt about who did it!

As I'm writing this, I'm looking out over the Gulf Coast. I'm here with my family for our yearly vacation. Literally as I write these words I'm sitting on a balcony listening to the waves crash onto the shore of the white sand beach. In this setting, I've found that it's much easier to understand how big God is. I look at the beauty of the ocean and realize that it couldn't have been a result of happenstance. When I see the miles of beautiful beaches, I realize that it wasn't an accident that it looks the way it does.

Have you ever considered how many gallons of water are in the ocean? How about the number of grains of sand that are in just one mile of beach? What about the number of fish in the ocean, and how do they find enough to eat in all that water? It can make your head hurt to consider how beautiful and complex the earth is. It also can make you realize that God is so much bigger than what we realize.

I would encourage you to get away, if that's what it takes, for you to refocus on the enormity of God. Do whatever it takes to rekindle your understanding that you have a God who loves you and wants the best for you. He's working on your behalf even right now.

God is Big

God is bigger than all sicknesses and diseases. He's bigger than every demand the world puts on us. He's bigger than every bill that comes your way. He's bigger than your failures and limitations. To limit God in saying things like, "God, you can part the Red Sea, and allow the children of Israel to escape on dry ground to escape from slavery, but after hearing what the doctor said, I don't know if you're able to heal my body."

God is bigger than what the doctors say and what the charts say. God is bigger than everything people tell you about a disease. The simple truth is this: God is bigger. When we realize this and put our faith in a great, big, enormous God who's able to do exceedingly and abundantly above all that we ever ask or think, I promise you that your life will be radically changed for the better.

Chapter Three: God Is Bigger Than Your Past

The Apostle Paul Had a Past

Everybody has a past. Life and time guarantee it. Based on how we view things, the past can haunt us or help us. The choice becomes ours. We find a man in the Bible named Paul, who was really quite a significant figure. In fact, he's responsible for writing most of the New Testament through the leading of the Holy Spirit. One of the books he wrote was II Corinthians. II Corinthians was a letter that Paul wrote to refute the argument people were making against him and his claims of being an apostle.

After Paul left Corinth, his travels took him through Ephesus where word got back to him that there were some around Corinth stirring people up and starting rumors about him. They were blasting him over his past and claiming that he really was not a man of God at all.

Whether we like it or not, people do that sort of thing. People will attack your integrity by attacking your past. People will bring your past into the present and judge you based only on what happened years before. Those darts and arrows of judgment and criticism hurt. And perhaps you have a past of which you're not proud. Maybe you're still struggling with the pain, rejection and sins of the past. But whether you've experienced a radical transformation and you've conquered the past, or if you're still trying to untangle and straighten out your life, God is bigger than the past. And it can be so unfair when no matter how much you change and how much you prove, people are stuck on your past mistakes. That's when you have to know that God is big enough to take care of your past.

As Paul was being slandered, demeaned and insulted, perhaps some of those people were bringing his past into the present. Perhaps some of them knew the old Paul. The truth be told, before he met the Lord on the road to Damascus, Paul was a pretty nasty guy. Some of Paul's enemies may have been digging up his past and throwing it in his face. Paul was going around talking about being righteous before God, but there may have been those who knew the things Paul was involved in before he became a follower of Christ.

After all, this was the man who stood by and watched as men picked up boulders and stoned to death a young believer named Stephen. They could have recognized him to be one of the young up and coming religious leaders who wanted to impress his superiors at every turn by harassing the Christ followers into humiliation and submission. They may have remembered his name was originally Saul, but this was the same man who would go on murderous rampages killing Christians, being responsible for their deaths. This same man, now known as Paul, would obtain letters from the magistrates empowering him to go after, arrest, and imprison those who followed Christ. This sounds like a dangerous, zealous, ego-maniac out to make a name for himself in the world.

And just imagine someone with his past reputation coming into your church and wanting to get involved as a volunteer or teacher. If someone with this kind of a past came into the congregation, we would have the temptation to do like the Corinthians and bring his past into the present to judge him according to what he had done before being intro-duced to Jesus. We have to guard ourselves from being judg-mental in that way. But there's something else that's just as important. We have to guard ourselves from letting people do that to us. Because the truth is this: if you've given your life to Jesus your past no longer matters to God. He has accepted you and forgiven you. In His eyes, He sees you like He sees Christ.

That's hard for people to understand, because, we remember our past. More than anyone else, we remember all the poor decisions we made, the things we said and did to people that's left a stain in our memories. We were there when it happened. And if we're not careful, we'll allow shame to depress us and we'll allow other people to judge us because of our past. We'll tuck our tail between our legs and duck our heads and never do anything for God because of what we did in the past.

One of the reasons that Paul was writing this letter to the Corinthian church was because people were trying to disqualify his authority because of things that happened in the past. This happened in other cities where Paul preached the gospel, too. People would go around town and spread rumors and lies about him. There may have been some truth from the past that people would bring up, but there are always those who will exaggerate things to stir up the crowd.

Paul knew what he had done in the past. He didn't try to hide it. He called himself the "chief" of sinners, but if it had not been for the blood of Christ and the grace of God, Paul would have had no way to answer his critics. If a person did take a look at his past, they would see that he was a pretty bad guy. But now in Christ, Paul stood on the reconciling and purifying power of God through the sacrifice of Jesus Christ on the cross. Paul knew he had no grounds or basis of his own works or his awful past to stand on to be right before God. He knew it was the saving work of Christ in his life. But this didn't matter to the people who wanted to tear Paul down.

Paul had done vile things in his past life. He did things that he couldn't be proud of, things that may have kept him up at night. He may have had a past memory flash across his mind about things that he wished he could take back. Perhaps you've been in that same frame of mind at some time. I would imagine that every one of us at some point in life have done things, have said things, or have acted in such ways that we wish we could go back and change it all.

You might even remember conversations where the words weren't even out of your mouth yet, but it's like you were powerless to stop it, and before you knew it you were regretting what you had just said. But by then it had already happened. It became part of your past that you wish you could change. The truth is, everybody has a past. We have things that we wish we could take back. And if people were to only look at our past and judge our effectiveness for God based upon what we've done in the past, virtually every single one of us would be counted unworthy to work for God.

That's exactly what Paul was dealing with. They were saying, "You're not a man of God. You're not an apostle. You're making all this up. You're only out for yourself." These accusers of Paul's didn't understand the powerful encounter that Paul had had with Christ. Just a short time back, somewhere on a dusty road, as Paul was going to Damascus to arrest Christians, to squash this new religion and to even murder them if he saw fit, something happened that would drastically alter his path for the future. He had an encounter with the true, living Christ who had been raised from the dead.

A Life Changing Encounter

We find this dramatic story in Acts 9 and it goes like this:

> *Now Saul, still breathing threats and murder against the disciples of the Lord, went to the high priest, and asked for letters from him to the synagogues at Damascus, so that if he found any belonging to the Way, both men and women, he might bring them bound to Jerusalem. As he was*

traveling, it happened that he was approaching Damascus, and suddenly a light from heaven flashed around him; and he fell to the ground and heard a voice saying to him, "Saul, Saul, why are you persecuting Me?" And he said, "Who are You, Lord?" And He said, "I am Jesus whom you are persecuting, but get up and enter the city, and it will be told you what you must do." The men who traveled with him stood speechless, hearing the voice but seeing no one. Saul got up from the ground, and though his eyes were open, he could see nothing; and leading him by the hand, they brought him into Damascus. And he was three days without sight, and neither ate nor drank.
Acts 9:1–9

Paul was zealous for God but didn't realize that he was in error. He needed to see things from a different viewpoint than he did in the past. Nothing like being blind for three days to change the way you see! God had to take Paul through this radical encounter where he lost his sight for a few reasons.

First, Paul needed to know the true Christ. In the days ahead God knew that Paul's faith would be tested. In those moments where people were doubting his call and calling into questions his motives, Paul had to be able to reflect on that specific moment where he met the risen Jesus on a dusty road to Damascus. The same is true for you and me. While we might not have the same experience that Paul had, we do need to encounter Christ on a personal level that leaves us forever changed. This encounter needs to take place for you and me for the same reason it did for Paul. People may question our motives and our ability to be used of God. If we aren't careful, we'll let those people start to convince us that it's possible we really can't be used of God. In these times, it's imperative that we can take our minds and hearts back to the spot where we first encountered Christ in a powerful way.

Secondly, Paul needed to know the power that was available to him as a believer. The story continues to tell of a man named Ananias. God spoke to Ananias about Paul and convinced him to go to the house where they had taken Paul in his blindness. Reluctantly, (because of Paul's reputation) Ananias followed the Lords instructions. The story in Acts goes on to tell us what happened next:

> But the Lord said to him, "Go, for he is a chosen
> instrument of Mine, to bear My name before the
> Gentiles and kings and the sons of Israel; for I will
> show him how much he must suffer for My name's

sake." So Ananias departed and entered the house, and after laying his hands on him said, "Brother Saul, the Lord Jesus, who appeared to you on the road by which you were coming, has sent me so that you may regain your sight and be filled with the Holy Spirit." And immediately there fell from his eyes something like scales, and he regained his sight, and he got up and was baptized; and he took food and was strengthened. Acts 9:15-19

Can you imagine Paul's surprise through all of this? Not only had he encountered the Christ, who He didn't believe had been raised from the dead, but now a mere man was healing him from blindness. Talk about something you would never forget! But, that's exactly why God did it that way. God needed Paul to know that through the name of Jesus, believers had extraordinary abilities.

Third, God needed Paul to fully understand His forgiveness. God knew that in coming days Paul would be tempted to let his mind wonder, "Was I really forgiven?" This is a tactic of the enemy that is as old as time itself. If the devil can get you to question who you are in Christ and whether you are really forgiven, he can get you to question God's existence all together. So, now that God had Paul's full attention, it became apparent in the succeeding chapters in Acts, that Paul came to understand the forgiveness of Christ. In conjunction, Paul began to understand – as I hope you will – that God is bigger than your past!

Do you believe that? Do you believe that God is BIG enough to forgive you of all of your past? Do you believe that you don't have to carry shame or guilt? That you don't have to feel condemned or inferior? That you don't have to drop your head down, and you don't have to tell yourself you can't do anything for God? If you're in Christ, all your sins are entirely forgiven and you can do all things through Christ which strengthens you! (Phil 4:13).

Paul had an encounter with Jesus and it changed him, and as an encounter with Christ should, it changed him forever. It should change you forever. You should never leave an encounter with Jesus and not be changed in a powerful way. We should desire such change every time we show up to church, or every time we read the Word, or spend time listening to worship music. Do you hunger to have that kind of encounter with Jesus and be changed? If so, you must allow Him to be bigger to you than your past.

It's in times like these that you can release your past to a God who's mighty enough to remove it from you. This is where you can allow yourself to receive forgiveness and be free of the opinions of people who might be judging your past. God's opinion of you is bigger than their opinions. His thoughts about you are better than the thoughts of others toward you. While others try to hold your past against who you are today, remember that God is bigger than your past. When He sees you in Christ, He sees you with a past that's cleansed of sin.

We All Have a Past

As I mentioned before, it can be said that we all have some sort of past. Maybe some of us have really checkered pasts, like me. Maybe we have things in our past that we've done that are really bad things. And unfortunately, people like to dig those things up. They don't necessarily like to talk about their past, but they do like to speak of yours.

People will try to judge us because of our past. They'll limit us because of our past. And quite honestly, we'll limit ourselves because of our past. But when we've had an encounter with Jesus Christ, we can say as the apostle Paul did to that Corinthian church in II Corinthians 5:17-21.

> *Therefore if anyone is in Christ, he's a new creation. The old has passed away; behold, the new*

has come. All this is from God who through Christ reconciled us to Himself, and gave us the testimony of reconciliation that is in Christ. God was reconciling the world to Himself, not counting their trespasses against them, and entrusting to us the message of reconciliation.

Look at verse 20: "So we are ambassadors for Christ. God making this appeal through us, we besiege you on behalf of Christ, be reconciled to God. For our sake, He made Him (Jesus) to be sin, who knew no sin, so that in Him, we might become the righteousness of God."

The "we," that He's talking about – which becomes the righteousness of God – is you and me. God's plan was worked out so that we might become righteous before Him, not through our own strength and not based on anything that we've done. We're righteous through Christ, not because our past is great, or because our past is horrible, but because of His sacrifice. The blood of Jesus Christ washes away all sin and makes things brand new.

Listen again to what Paul is saying here. "Therefore if anyone…" If anyone! Are you an anyone? I'm an anyone. You're an anyone. Paul is reminding us that any person on the face of this planet, who is in Christ, IS a new creation. Old things have passed away. All things have become new.

This is the good news of the Gospel. If you are in Christ, God has taken your sin and He's thrown it as far as the east is from the west. He doesn't even remember the sin that you try to keep bringing up to yourself. He doesn't remember the sin that other people are trying to bring up to you. He doesn't put stock in any of the things that are limiting you. He doesn't regard the things that are trying to condemn you. God doesn't even remember it.

If you're in Christ, God is so much bigger than your past. Think about it: God is way bigger than your sin, far bigger than your past, and He's more than big enough to forgive you forever. He cannot only forgive you but He can wipe away your past.

People were trying to discredit Paul, and people are going to attempt to discredit you. You're reading a book written by a minister that used to be a drug dealer. I have a past that God has completely forgiven me of forever. I know what Jesus has done for me. I know that I was like Paul. I was one of those guys that was the worse, most vile, sinning, kind of hard core person that would hit you in the shins with a lead pipe and would laugh about it. That's what kind of person I used to be.

But everything changed when I had an encounter with Jesus Christ, and when I had an encounter with the God who loved me so much that not only would He forgive me, I would feel forgiven. When I had that encounter, as Paul did, I bought into it fully. I gave myself over to believing that if anyone is in Christ, he's a new creation, old things have passed away and all things have become new. Because of what Jesus did for me and in me, I'm brand new.

If people try to judge you because of your past, you need to remind yourself, "Old things have passed away. Behold, I've been made brand new because I'm in Christ." Memorize II Corinthians 5:17. When people try to bring up your past against you, just remember that God doesn't hold your past against you anymore because you are in Christ. Just remember that He cast your sin as far as the east is from the west, because you are in Christ. Romans 8:1 says, "There is therefore now no condemnation to those who are in Christ."

Every time the enemy begins to tell me, "You're a failure or you're going under," I remind myself that, "There is therefore now no condemnation to those who are in Christ, so devil, you might as well shut your mouth, because I'm in Christ." The enemy will try to whisper dumb little things in your mind and try to make you feel condemned or even like the worst kind of failure. Remind yourself, "My Father doesn't talk that way to me. There's no condemnation to me because I am in Christ. God is merciful to me and His mercies are new every morning. He promised that He will be merciful to my unrighteousness, and my sins and iniquities He will remember no more because I'm in Christ."

Please hear the heart of what I'm saying here. God is bigger than your past! God is not going to hold your past against you.

I think about "pasts" like I think about "comb overs." I can speak about comb overs from firsthand experience because my hair's getting a little thin in the back. It all starts very subtly. You start trying to force some hair to cover up most of the bald spot. A little hairspray here, a little gel there, and before you know it you've successfully convinced yourself that no one will ever notice all that skin showing under those few strands of hair.

People take this same tactic in dealing with their past mistakes. They try to do a spiritual "comb over" thinking that everyone will think they were born with a beautiful head of hair and it has always looked this way. But the truth is, the spot we're trying to cover up is still there. You can't hide it in a way that it's never seen again. Everybody has a past. Everybody has sinned and fallen short of God's standard for our lives. And sin is sin. We try to rate one sin over another, but to God it's all the same. So it doesn't matter what you're sin is, to be in Christ we all need God's forgiveness.

The problem is one of recognition. There are things that need to be recognized in order for God to be personally bigger to us than our past. There are things that we need to recognize about ourselves. There are things about our thinking, which must be recognized in order that we can be totally free and feel completely forgiven about our past. One of the places of wrong thinking that must be addressed is the person who says, "I don't need His forgiveness." People who think this way are trying to pretend their past isn't really there.

I Don't Need His Forgiveness

To have a past you've not released to the Lord is like the guy who starts with a little comb over to try and hide the fact that he does have a past. People tend to think that they don't have as raw and rough a past as a drug dealer, an alcoholic or an addict, but people have other things that are just as repulsive to God. God hates pride. God hates discord. God hates gossip. Yet how many people have walked in these ways for years and think that it's not as harsh as these other things mentioned?

Romans 3:23 says, "All have sinned and come short of the glory of God." My sin may be "worse" than yours from the looks of things, but the truth is that sin is sin. And we've all sinned. We've all done things and said things that at some point in our lives were disobedient to God. "But you don't understand. I'm a really good person." It's the number one answer I get when we're witnessing on the street. Anytime I share with somebody about Christ and I ask them, "Do you think you're going to make it into heaven?" They'll say, "I'm a pretty good person," as though being a good person gets you into heaven. The reason I bring that up is because I used to think that. I thought that for a long time – that just being a good person would get me into heaven. But then it dawned on me one day, "How good is good enough? How do I know when good is good enough to get into heaven?"

God wouldn't be a very loving or fair God if He said, "Well, good luck. Do the best you can." The truth is that, whether you think you need God's forgiveness or not, whether you're a good person or you think you're a good person or not, we all need Christ's forgiveness. Isaiah 64:6 says that, "We all have become like him who is unclean. And all our righteous deeds are like a polluted garment. We all fade like a leaf, and our iniquities, like the wind, take us away." We all have a past.

We all have sinned at some point in our life. James 4:17 says, "Whoever knows what is right to do and fails to do it, for him it is sin."

That boils it down to very simple terms. If you've ever done anything in your life that you know was not the right thing to do, you've sinned. That's pretty heavy. It's heavy to think about the fact that every person needs Christ's forgiveness. So really the argument of "I don't need God's forgiveness," doesn't stand because everyone on the face of the earth has done something wrong at some point in our lives and need God's forgiveness.

God Can't or Won't Forgive Me

And then there's another type of person that says, "God can't or won't forgive me. I've done terrible, horrible, vile, wicked things like Paul. I've done things that nobody even knew I did them. They're terrible, terrible things. How could God ever forgive me?"

If you're the person who thinks that God can't or won't forgive you, what I would tell you to do is look at John 3:17. "For God sent the Son into the world, not to condemn the world, but that the world might be saved through Him." God didn't send Jesus to the earth to live a perfect life, die on a cross, and be raised from the dead on the third day, so that you could struggle through life wondering if you're saved. He did that so you could place your faith in a God who can forgive you *no matter what*. No matter what you've ever done, there's not a sin that you can commit that's never been committed before. Have you ever thought about that? There's not one sin that you could dream up to do that's going to make God stand up in wonder in amazement, dumbfounded at a new sin.

For the theologians reading this, we're not going to get into the blasphemy of the Holy Spirit and the unpardonable sin. What I'm talking about is if you have a consciousness that God is alive and able to forgive, but that He won't forgive you, that's wrong. He will forgive you. He will forgive you no matter what you've done.

You may think you don't deserve a second chance. God is more than willing to give you a second chance. God will forgive you. II Chronicles 30:9 says:

> *For if you return to the Lord, your brethren and your children will find compassion with their captors, and return to this land. For the Lord your God is gracious and merciful and will not turn away His face from you, if you return to Him.*

All through the Bible, people who have humbled themselves

and realized that they need the forgiveness of God, and have gone to this mighty, loving God, He's forgiven them every time.

Not Forgiving Yourself

But once people realize they need God's forgiveness, perhaps the biggest hurdle they have to jump is forgiving themselves. The people you hurt may have already forgiven you, so stop replaying the past over and over again in your head. It's time to shake off the past and forgive yourself. You may not have felt that God would allow you to be used to serve Him, but the truth is that God can use you. He uses people with broken pasts. I think He likes it when somebody who's been all messed up in their life receives His forgiveness and makes up their mind that they're going to do great things for Him.

But to do great things for Him, God needs you to forgive yourself. If you've struggled to forgive yourself, Hebrews 9:14 will help you do so. "How much more shall the blood of Christ, who through the eternal Spirit offered Himself without blemish to God, purify your conscience." The blood of Christ purifies your conscience from dead works to serve the living God. Hebrews 10:22 says, "Let us draw near with a true heart in full assurance of faith with our hearts sprinkled clean from an evil conscience." Through His blood, Jesus has made it possible to have a clear, clean conscience and heart.

If you've been holding on to your past year after year, it's time to let it go and be sprinkled clean from a tormented conscience. Imagine how free you'll feel by letting God take your past from you. Imagine the things that would change in your life and the victory you could walk in. God is bigger than your pasts and He is powerful enough to also help you feel forgiven. It may be hard to receive but it's the truth.

The Big Key to Living Bigger

The people who have received God's forgiveness in their lives have learned a great key to living bigger in life. God became bigger than their past. They've placed their faith in a risen Christ and allowed the power of Christ's blood to flow through them, work through them, and restore all the brokenness on the inside of them. They've received Jesus' sacrifice as their pardon from sin and choose to live as though their past cannot be held against them.

You have things that God has placed on your heart. God is birthing vision in you and perhaps He's spoken to you about ideas, business ventures, ministries, and things to do wherever He's called you to serve, but you've been allowing your past to keep you chained down from serving Him. This is your time to be released into the future of your dreams. Allow the blood of Jesus Christ to cleanse your conscience, let go of your past and step into God's mercy and grace.

Chapter Four: God Is Bigger Than Your Pain

Regardless of what you need at this very moment, whether it's a financial miracle, restoration in your marriage, a miracle of healing, or if you have emotional pain, we serve a God that's big enough to take care of all of your problems. There was a man in the Old Testament who faced his share of emotional turmoil and in each instance he turned to God. King David was known as a man after God's own heart. But when we look at the life of David, we see a man who at various times in his life rode an emotional rollercoaster.

In Psalm 31 David wrote about a time when he feared for his life. In this Psalm David prayed to God and God sent help. A little later in this Psalm he voiced another request for help and God responded again. On more than one occasion, David ran for his life to escape from the clutches of King Saul. Psalm 31:9-13 describes what David felt during the times when he was being pursued by Saul and his armies.

> *Be gracious to me, O Lord, for I am in distress. My eye is wasted from grief. My soul and my body also, for my life is spent with sorrow, and my years with sighing. My strength fails me because of my misery, and my bones waste away. I am the scorn of all my adversaries, a horror to my neighbors, an object of dread to my acquaintances. Those who see me in the street flee from me. I have passed out of my mind like one who is dead. I have become like a broken vessel. I hear the whisper of many, terror on every side as they scheme together against me, and as they plot to take my life.*

David sounds like he's right on the verge of a breakdown. This is a man who Saul tried to kill on multiple occasions. Saul had trusted David as a warrior on the battlefield. David had served Saul admirably time after time, but now the king of Israel had become his enemy. David was isolated from all that was familiar to him, chased across the countryside, living in mountainous terrain, hiding in caves.

David understood emotional pain. David understood hardship. He understood what it was like to have people turn their backs on him. When David was just a youth, he went to the battlefront where his brothers were fighting in the army against the Philistines. Upon his arrival at the battle site, he began to ask those around him about the taunts of the giant Goliath. He asked what would happen to the man that defeated this man named Goliath. And his own brothers began to ridicule him and accuse him of having a wicked and conceited heart. His own family turned against him.

Later Saul, whom David looked up to as his king, got so jealous of David that he threw a spear at David trying to pin him to the wall. David loved Saul, but he felt the emotional pain of betrayal by someone who should have been a mentor.

Later on, David's own son, Absalom, turned his back on him and tried to overthrow David's kingship. Absalom was angered that David had seemingly done nothing after Absalom's sister, Tamar, had been raped by one of David's other sons. David had forgiven Absalom but refused to see his face. David was a man who had emotional dysfunction that plagued his family many different times.

Then, because of David's own sin, he saw the loss of a

child. If there was anybody who had the excuse to be depressed in life, it was David. This mighty man, who was after God's own heart, had experienced those closest to him turning their backs on him. His own family hurt him. His friends deserted him and he grieved over the death of loved ones. If you're suffering with depression and emotional pain, David would have understood, because he was just like you in that he had emotional pain.

He knew what it was like to have hardships happening in his life. And the truth is, he could have grown very bitter if he wanted to. He could have begun to feel sorry for himself and to be bitter at how other people treated him. He could have blamed God and talked about what he thought God had done to him. He could have been bitter because of the people that didn't recognize his authority as king.

Most every one of us has had the temptation to feel that same kind of bitterness about things that happened to us in our lives. Most every one of us could tell of how someone close, maybe even a family member, has turned their back on you. Perhaps you could tell all about how people have been accusing you of things that you didn't say and didn't do. Maybe you could tell how friends deserted you. You could speak from personal experience of what it's like to carry the pain that's inflicted from those closest to you.

Everyone at some point in life has carried emotional pain. And it hurts, doesn't it? It's that kind of pain that's really hard to deal with because it's not like having a doctor put a cast on a broken arm that can heal in several weeks. It's a deep kind of emotional, inside pain that nobody can see, but can last far longer than a few days or weeks. Many times we try to hide it. We can put on a smiling face and walk around trying to pretend like nothing's happening in our lives. The truth is that people experience all kinds of emotional pain during their lifetime. But God is bigger than our pain. He can help us deal with it.

People can start to feel there is no hope. They feel like their emotional baggage is a heavy load that's pushed all hope away. There is hope if we'll put our faith into a BIG God. We have to realize what emotional stress, and emotional baggage is doing to our lives. It leaves us emotionally drained, spiritually depleted, and feeling despair. Obviously, we're not at our best when we're emotionally drained. It leaves us physically exhausted.

Scientists and doctors have even proven that carrying emotional pain and toxic emotions can cause physical ailments. It's important that we figure out a way to deal with the pain in our lives, because if we hold onto it, it will cause us physical pain.

And what impact does emotional pain have on us spiritually? Spiritually, when we're carrying around emotional pain, it keeps us and our families from being what God wants us to be. So the question is, "Can there really be a place of hope in the midst of emotional pain?" Is there hope for you that this emotional pain, that perhaps you've carried around for years, can be relieved? The answer is yes, but you've got to know how to do it.

The Master Watch Maker

When I was just a very small boy, maybe eight years old, my stepfather used to take me to my Uncle Homer's watch shop. It was just a storefront kind of shop located in a small town, but in this shop there were clocks and watches everywhere you looked. The best clocks for an eight year old boy were the cuckoo clocks. Boy, did he have plenty of those! I loved the cuckoo clocks. He had them all set at the same time, so at noon, for instance, they were all cuckooing at the same time. My uncle understood how each one of them worked, so if they malfunctioned, he had the expertise to make them work right.

In that watch shop, I could remember thinking, "Wow. Look at all these watches. There must be a lot of people with broken watches; there must be very few people who know how to fix watches." Uncle Homer would take a magnifying glass, and put it in front of his eye, and hold one of those pocket watches real close. Then he took his tiny little tools and changed the small moving parts. He knew exactly what a watch needed, no matter how broken it was.

In the same way, God knows exactly what you need to fix the broken areas that have caused you emotional pain. You can go to everyone else in the world to try to get healing for that pain, but the place you need to go is into the hands of the One who created your innermost being.

God is the One who's BIG enough to change out all your parts to make you brand new. God is like a Master Watch Maker, and not just for the twenty-first century, but for all time and eternity. Regardless of how much pain or hurt you've carried, God knows exactly what you need, because He is a BIG God. II Corinthians 1 tells us that God is the Father of mercies and He's the God of all comfort who comforts us in all of our affliction.

So what do we do in order to be partakers of the mercies and comfort of God? Going back to David in Psalm

31, let's look at what we can learn about pain and how he responded to it.

In this psalm, David is baring his soul to God and pouring out his complaint before the Lord in the fashion of a prayer. In a very transparent manner, David is speaking from the depths of his heart the things that are most weighing on him. He's uttering to God his emotional pain. He tells God that everybody on every side had turned their back on him, including his family. David was saying he was a wounded spirit, and that his bones were like dust. He was in that dry place where it seemed nothing gave any rhyme or reason to his life. In essence, he was saying that he felt like he could just lie down and die. At that moment, David wasn't in a very good place emotionally. But then something changed. He began to remember the Lord and verbalized his trust in the Lord. He remembered where his help came from. He brought to his attention the faithfulness of God to deliver him in so many other hard places. His reflections take him to the place where he could voice his trust in God. And even though all these bad things were happening and he was carrying all of this emotional baggage, betrayal, and hurt, David gets to the place of saying, "I trust in You, O Lord. You are my God."

An important lesson to learn is that a great deal of

coming out of emotional pain is centered around how big you make your problems out to be and what you say about your problems. Notice that David said, "You are my God. My times are in thy hand. Deliver me from the hand of my enemies and persecutors. Let Your face shine on your servant. Save me by Your steadfast love. Let me not be put to shame, O Lord, for I call on You. Let the wicked be put to shame. Let them be dumbfounded to Sheol. Let the lying lips of the dumb which speak insolently against the righteous in pride and contempt be put to silence."

David said "I *say* You are my God." A lot of healing from emotional pain comes from what you say about God. I want you to realize this truth. To overcome emotional pain and the baggage that goes with it, you have to release the pain and rely on the promise.

Doing that can be very difficult for people, especially when they're going around and complaining to everyone they know about all the problems going on in their lives. When you voice all the problems that are going on in your life to everybody who'll listen, you may feel a temporary sense of relief, but it usually isn't long before any measure of relief gives way to an increase of misery. When you say things like, "I'm never going to get over this," or "Those people have hurt me so bad that I never can forgive them," you're speaking contradictory to the truth of God's Word. You can't speak against God's Word and expect to get His results or promises.

Releasing the Pain, Relying On the Promise

David said, "I say You are my God. Even though all of these things are happening, You are my God." We have to determine that God is bigger than our pain. He's bigger than anything that you're dealing with right now. Start to believe right now that God is bigger than your pain. And you need to start saying that, because when you say it over and over and over and over, faith begins to rise up on the inside of you. When that emotional pain tries to come against you, you'll be right there with the King of kings, and the Lord of lords hand in hand as He walks you through this pain. It starts and builds momentum because you choose to say, "You are my God!"

A big part of releasing the pain begins with what you say. What you say helps you to release the pain and rely on the promises of God's word. Pain is temporary, but the promises of God are forever. I know that right now it seems like the pain that you're dealing with is never going to end. I'm telling you it's going to end if you'll release that pain to God and rely on His promises. He's a BIG God. He can take care of what you're dealing with right now.

Matthew 12:34, it says, "For out of the abundance of the heart the mouth speaks." This isn't just about making positive confessions. This is about truthful declaring. If you say something that's contradictory to God's Word, you are lying about yourself. Did you get that? Go back and read that sentence again.

God's Word doesn't say things like, *You're not going to have a hope or a future.* God doesn't say that you're going to have to deal with this pain forever. But He does say that He has made you the head of things and not the tail. God does promise that even though the righteous face afflictions, He will deliver us out of them all. God does promise that in Christ, He always causes us to triumph. We may face problems, but He promises that greater is He that is in us than he that is in the world. Though fear may come against us, and weapons may form against us, He does promise that He's not given us a spirit of fear but of power, love, and a sound mind. He promises that no weapon formed against us will prosper. Relying on the promises through what you say will release the pain.

This isn't merely a form of positive thinking. This is called faith. Out of the abundance of the heart the mouth speaks. Proverbs 18:21 says that "death and life are in the power of the tongue." It's important to know, that if you're saying something that's contrary to the Word, you're lying about yourself and inviting death, or separation, from the life God promised. It's time to begin to speak truth and life over yourself. Speak the truth of God's Word that contains the life of God's Spirit.

Unfortunately, here's what people do. Somebody hurts them or they have some type of altercation with a family member, or a disagreement with somebody at school, work, or in the church, and they go home and replay that scenario in their mind over and over. They rehearse what was said and how people responded and they watch the event in their mind's eye refreshing the screen again and again.

Have you ever left a confrontation and thought about everything you should have said? Did you think about all the witty and biting remarks you could have launched against the other person? Did you tell somebody else about how wrong the person was that you're at odds with? It's not long before you've got a feature-length movie going on inside of your head that doesn't belong there. If you want to release the pain, you've got to change the scenery in your mind and in your thoughts. And when you do that, things that come out of your mouth will change, too. When you change the pictures and scenery within you, that's when you are rehearsing what God says about you in the Word.

In Psalm 31:19, David goes on to say, "O, how abundant is Your goodness which You have laid up for those who fear You, and wrought for those who take refuge in You." When you remember the goodness of the Lord, it becomes a safe dwelling place for your soul. Allowing your mind to rehearse and replay all God's goodness brings refreshing, restoration, and strength to your soul. And when your soul is strengthened like this, it becomes much easier to release the pain and rely on His promises.

Run To a Safe Place

Listen again to what David says in Psalm 31. "For those who take refuge in You, in the sight of the sons of men, in the covert of Your presence, You hide them from the plots of men. You hold them under Your shelter from the strife of their tongue." Many people try to run from their pain by running from God to drugs, alcohol, and immorality. But the place to run is to God and to the safe place He provides.

To be free of emotional pain, first of all, you need to release that pain by relying on the promises. The next step toward emotional healing is being able to run to that safe place. You need to know where that is and what that is. The world will try to sell you a bill of goods about this and that – do this program, buy this book, join this club. You can do that all you want, but you'll never find a true, lasting shelter and place of safety unless you're wrapped in the arms of Jesus Christ. He is the Prince of Peace. He is the One who cares for you, who loves you so much that He would die and take your place on the cross of consequence. How in the world could someone in this life love you more than that? He loves you and cares for you, and will protect you more than anybody else. He is the safe place.

Traumatic Weather

Some time ago, we had some pretty traumatic weather in my home state of Oklahoma. (Come to think of it we are always having traumatic weather in Oklahoma!) Anyway, as the biggest tornado in the state was ripping through the western side of the city, we felt we needed to get to a friend's home that had a storm shelter. As we were driving to the shelter, we were literally driving straight into the storm. It was the most vicious lightning I've ever seen in my entire life. The sky was pitch black and wicked looking. Finally we made it into the shelter and felt safe.

I tell you that story to emphasize that God is the only shelter that's powerful enough and big enough to protect you from every danger in life. You may be driving right into the middle of the biggest storm you've ever faced in your entire life. He's the shelter. He's the safest place you can be in any storm. There's no other place in this world that will offer you the sense of security, protection and safety like this God who's big enough to cover you at all times. If you're in a storm, run to the safe place. Don't run *from* Jesus Christ, run *to* Him.

You can be saved from emotional pain. God will be with you and walk you through the pain to the place of safety. Proverbs 18:10 says that, "The name of the Lord is a strong tower; the righteous man runs into it and he is safe." If you want to be saved from emotional pain, run to the safe place.

Remain Faithful

David goes on in Psalm 31:21-24, saying,

> *Blessed be the Lord, for He has wondrously shown His steadfast love to me when I was beset in a besieged city. I had said in my alarm, I am driven far from Your sight, but You heard my supplications when I cried to You for help. Love the Lord*

all you saints. The Lord preserves the faithful, but abundantly requites him who acts haughtily. Be strong and let your heart take courage all you who wait for the Lord.

Look at what David says: "He preserves the faithful." So not only do you need to release that pain and rely on the promises, not only do you need to remain in that safe place, but when you get there you've got to remain faithful. You have to stay there. He said that God preserves the faithful.

In the Greek, the word "preserves" means "to guard and to protect." It literally means that God guards and protects the faithful. So we could say, "The Lord protects the faithful." It also means "to maintain." God maintains the faithful.

Everything else in your life could be crumbling apart, but if you'll remain in Him and you'll remain faithful, He'll keep a guard over you and protect you. He'll sustain you through hardship. If you stay faithful, He'll maintain you. You need to stay faithful to entering into His presence on a daily basis. On a daily basis enter into His presence with a heart of thanksgiving. Stay faithful to His promises. Pick up His Word, and read it not out of obligation or because someone is telling you to do it, but because your love for Him has grown to the point that you can't help but pick up His Word and find out what God wants to speak to you today.

The blessings and the mercies of God are brand new every day. His mercies are new and fresh every single day. Every day you can pick up the Word of God and He will speak to you some truth that's for you that day. His Word is alive. It's living and active and sharper than any two edged sword. Stay faithful to His promises. But in order to stay faithful to His promises, you have to know them. And it's an amazing thing to experience, because the more you know His promises, the more you will come to love Him, and you even realize how much He loves you. Then your love for Him will grow exponentially. It is like compound interest; it's genuinely amazing.

How about staying faithful to His house? The Bible says to not forsake the assembling of ourselves together as some people do. What we need to do is to stay tight together. We need to stay tight together in God's house, because the fellowship of believers doing life together will strengthen you to stay faithful.

Two Ways God Relieves Pain

John 19 tells us of when Jesus was hanging on that cross. He looked down at His disciples, and to His mother, Mary, and

He said to His mother, Mary, "Dear woman, here is your son." And to the disciple John, He said, "Here is your mother." One of the ways that God speaks to us to relieve pain is through people. God relieves the emotional pain that we carry around and He uses people to do it. People are the ones who may hurt us, but isn't it interesting that it's also people who God uses to help heal us and relieve us of pain.

The very thing that hurts us is the very thing that God will use to help heal us. The enemy will try to tell you that you can never trust people again. He will try to tell you to put up walls and barriers, wear masks behind which to hide from people. God says trust Him and He'll show you the people to trust. God says open your heart, let down the walls, take off the mask, and trust people again. If you'll trust Him, He's big enough to show you who those "safe" people are. The people who are okay to go to, and who you can trust to let into your life.

Let me ask you a question: the first time you tried to ride a bike and you crashed, did you quit riding your bike? Most people would say no. And I say the same thing to you about people. Don't give up on all people just because one, or two, or even several people hurt you.

I don't know what that person did to you. I don't know

how their words hurt you. I don't know the abuses you've suffered. I don't know how people have mistreated you. But for every person that's ever hurt you, God has many more who you can be introduced to who will care for you, accept you, lift you up and love you for exactly who you are.

This only takes place if you don't give up on people just because one hurt you. Just because a few people didn't do you right, don't give up on all people. If you're willing to be reachable, there are places you can go within your church that have small groups of believers who will stand with you through your storms and love you with pure hearts like you have never been loved.

You may not have had a dad who was there for you, but God will help you find a Godly dad figure. God wants you to find that couple who would be like grandparents. You'll find brothers and sisters who love you. They'll be the ones who will cry with you, and hold your hand, and pour prayers over you.

Healing of the Holy Spirit

The second way that God uses to heal emotional pain is through the Holy Spirit. John 14:15 says, "If you love Me keep My commandments, and I will pray the Father and He shall give you another Comforter." Notice that word Comforter. "He will give you another Comforter, that He may abide with you forever." How does God heal emotional pain? How does God become bigger than your pain? Through people, and through the Holy Spirit. The Holy Spirit is a Person and He's bigger than your pain. Maybe you've never given Him a chance. Could it be that He really is bigger than your pain? Could it be that the Holy Spirit could comfort you during the suffering you are facing right now? The answer is a resounding YES!

The greatest example that I can give you for this is the young lady that my wife and I met two weeks after we became youth pastors several years ago. I had just finished Bible school and this church was crazy enough to hire me as their youth pastor in this small town in East Central Oklahoma.

We had actually just moved our household goods there and were in another city eating with some friends when we got the phone call. On the other end was this frantic voice and this young lady said to me, "Pastor Jerod. I think my brothers are dead."

I said, "Where are you?" She said, "I'm standing on the side of the road. We were going to Colorado to my brothers' wedding. And my two older brothers were in front of us and they got way ahead of us, and we came up on a car wreck, and we stopped…and it's my brothers. They won't let me go up there, but I think they're dead."

A drunk driver had come across the highway and took the entire top of the car off. Emergency crews were coming and she watched as they laid sheets across her brothers' bodies. I'd been a youth pastor for two weeks. Two weeks! I didn't know what to tell this young girl. I just said, "Listen, God loves you. And I don't understand why bad things happen. But I know that we serve a BIG God who will help you through this."

A few years later, during her senior year of high school, I got another call from this same young lady. "They said my dad's not going to make it. He's going to come home because he wants to die at home."

And I was there at the house just a few seconds after her father took his last breath. He was a friend. What do you tell somebody at that moment? All I could say was, "Listen, we serve a BIG God. And I don't understand why bad things happen. But we serve a BIG God who will help you through this."

I remember the day that she sat in my office and she told me, "I'm having to take care of my sisters all by myself. I'm doing all the cooking. I'm doing all the cleaning, because my mom is addicted to prescription pain medication. She's not taking care of us." What do you say? I don't know. I just said, "We serve a BIG God, He will help you through this."

This young lady had two paths that she could have taken. From the moment that she was standing on the side of a road, half way to Denver Colorado, she had a decision to make. She decided she was going to serve God through her pain. As a teenager, she decided that no matter what, she was going to believe that God's a BIG God.

This young lady has become our God Daughter. I've had very few moments in my life which made me more proud than what happened a few years ago. Even through all of the emotional pain she had to deal with, and although it seemed that everything was stacked up against her, just a few years ago my wife and I got to travel to Waco, Texas, and watch her walk across the stage at Baylor University to receive a Bachelor's Degree in Social Work. A few years after that, she finished a master's degree. This all worked out because she chose to believe that God was bigger than her pain.

I don't understand everything about why bad things happen to good people. But, I've seen God come through big time for people who are hurting. In Matthew 11:28, Jesus said, "Come to Me all you who labor and are heavy laden, and

I will give you rest." I Peter 5:7 says, "Cast all your anxieties on Him, for He cares about you." Colossians 3:15 tells us to, "Let the peace of Christ rule in your hearts."

God and His promises are bigger than your pain. He'll help you every step of the way. He'll help you during the times that you can't pick yourself up off the floor. He will help you when you are in the midst of your tears. He will help you through this pain. But you've got to be willing to let go of the pain and hang on to His promises. You've got to be willing to stay in the shelter under the wings of the Almighty God. And you've got to be willing to stay faithful to God and to let people and the Holy Spirit help you to heal beyond the pain.

Chapter Five: God Is Bigger Than Your Sickness

Hang-Ups About Healing

Biblical healing can be a controversial topic. When you study back through the centuries, we find that there have always been contending factions that have viewed the area of healing from different perspectives. There have been those on the side that believe God may allow sickness in some people's lives and heal others, but you couldn't know His will on the matter to understand who He's healing and who He's not healing. There have been those who believe God heals, but He may want some people to stay sick for some unknown reason. There are those who believe God heals all the time, and yet others who believe that healing is something Jesus did to prove His deity but that it all passed away with the death of the last of the original apostles.

Wherever you stand on the matter, I think there's one thing that we can clearly see from church history and from modern times: We have hang-ups about healing. We have those things, whether they be the traditions of men or something we heard a trusted minister or close relative say about the matter, that get us hung up on believing God for healing of the physical body.

For many, we've seen the good and we've seen the bad when it comes to teaching and ministering healing. We've seen preachers abuse the message of healing. We've gotten to the place where people were afraid to come to the altar because, quite honestly, they were afraid of how the preacher was going to act at the altar about healing. But the fact remains that among all these hang ups, we should look to the Word first, because God is still bigger than sickness, and He's bigger than all the hang ups about healing. He's still a healing God. Let's look at some of these hang ups.

Sickness to Teach a Lesson

One of the things that I've heard from people is, "I think God put this sickness on me to teach me a lesson." And people have really believed that. They've really believed this about God. I was in a situation one time where we were praying for a sick person—the person being prayed for wasn't present—and the person doing the praying said in their prayer, "And, Lord, if you've put this on them to try to teach them a lesson, I pray that they would learn that lesson quickly."

The scriptures and the Spirit of Truth are primary teachers of the Christian, and although there's much to be learned from our circumstances, God doesn't place sickness on a person as an object lesson in life. That would be like a parent putting flu antibodies in their child's cereal to teach them a lesson about washing dishes, or locking a child allergic to a bee sting in their room with a swarm of bees to teach them a lesson about cleaning up their room. Fear can be a powerful motivator, but God hasn't given us a spirit of fear, and He's certainly not using fear tactics as His primary modus operandi. When it comes to believing God for healing or anything else, I want to be filled with faith, not fear. When it comes right down to it, why else pray if we don't understand that God's the Healer and He wants to heal you?

We don't want to toss up our prayers and kind of hope that it hits God at just the right time. When we pray, this isn't the "healing lottery" and we're hoping to get the lucky, magic 8-ball ticket. When we pray, we don't have to hope God's having a good day and feels up to healing. We're in trouble if God and the devil are working together against us. God doesn't have arguments with Jesus, the Holy Spirit, and the angels, and then lose His temper and take His anger out on us. God's not like men. He doesn't think about how tired or bothered He is with all these healing needs. God doesn't make us wait and delay healing out of being mean, vindictive and spiteful.

No! That's not how God works. Rather, God is a healing, magnificently wonderful, BIG God who is bigger than all sicknesses and greater than all diseases. He's bigger! God is a BIG God. God did not put sickness on you. To say God is the one who decided to bring sickness into the earth and put it on His children is a lie from the father of lies. You have to settle the issue within yourself and resist the fallacy that God is crippler and destroyer of people's bodies. God is a good God. He's a merciful God and He's a BIG God.

Let's settle one theological point that has the inherent capacity to set you free from fear about sickness and calamity. Here it is, are you ready? Put your mind around this, because it's really deep. Ahem…okay…here goes.

Good God; bad devil.

Did you get that? Look back and read it again and again until it sinks in. I told you it was deep! God is a good God all the time, and the devil is a bad devil all the time. They don't change and they haven't swapped job titles or responsibilities. God stands for truth. The devil stands for deception. God perpetuates life. The devil perpetuates death. God stands for good. The devil stands for evil. God brings healing. The devil brings sickness. God is bigger than all the devil's wiles, schemes and strategies.

It's a simple thing to remember, but it's also a very profound thing to internalize. God is good, really good and He doesn't change. Our enemy's a liar, a compulsive liar, and he doesn't change. For some reason, that can be a hard concept for people to wrap their minds around, but it's the truth. Think about this a little further. Why would a good God put bad sickness on people? That doesn't make any sense. If you've been affected by this wrong way of thinking, you have to get past the thought that God puts sickness on you. It's hard to believe that God wants you well if you believe He's the One that made you sick. Imagine for the moment if God made you sick, and the devil is against you, too, where does your relief and healing come from? The bottom line is this: Sickness and disease did not originate from God. There is a different source for illness.

Who Is The Author Of Sickness And Disease?

Where did sickness come from? Think about it for a moment. In Genesis 2:17, God told His creation, whom He just created in a perfect environment, "But of the tree of the knowledge of good and evil you shall not eat from it. In the day that you eat from it you shall die."

God put a condition there. There was one tree out of the entire garden they were instructed to stay away from. Now remember, they could eat everything else but the fruit from this one tree. A few years ago, God showed me something interesting about this story. When you think about it, how many trees did they have to walk past to get to that one from which they couldn't eat? They had the whole garden. They had everything. God said, "Look around, it's all for you. But just that one thing I want you to stay away from."

Before that time there was no sickness, no illness, and no disease. So we can agree that up to this point, before Adam and Eve had fallen into sin, there was no sickness and no disease in the Garden of Eden. God had already created everything and then He rested from His work. He didn't rest because He was tired; He rested because He was finished!

Everything needful for man to live and experience His will was available to them and there is no mention of sickness, illness, or disease as part of God's plan.

What happened in the garden? The serpent came to Eve and said, "Did God really say you can't touch the tree of the knowledge of good and evil?" After being tempted and deceived by the serpent, man went to the tree of the knowledge of good and evil and ignored God's instructions. The serpent told Adam and Eve that if they ate from the forbidden tree they could be like God. The deception was to make them think they weren't already like God. God had made them in His image and after His likeness, and He gave them authority like God in the earth as the offspring of God. But they fell prey to the words of the serpent.

Remember all that we talked about before, about how God spoke and what He spoke then happened. God said, "Let there be light, and there was light." God said, "Don't eat from the tree of the knowledge of good and evil." And the enemy's strategy was to question what God said by saying, "Did God really say that you couldn't eat from this tree, too?" That's exactly where the enemy wants you – questioning. "Did God really say I could be healed?"

The enemy will tell you that the doctors went to school

for 12 years, they're smarter than you and they should know whether you can be healed or not. They know whether you're going to make it or not, whether you can live or not.

I have a lot of respect for doctors and we all should respect the work doctors are doing in medical research towards healing and preserving life. Doctors are very smart. They do understand complex things about the body and the healing process. But even doctors don't have the ultimate, final authority over who's healed or not, and who lives or dies. They can help facilitate healing and life, but health professionals didn't create the body and they don't know everything there is to know about how your body will best respond to treatments in order to be completely healed.

Physicians know some things about your body, but they can't make it from the dirt of the ground. They can't make an organ out of tissue just as God does. They can't form a body the way God formed a body. He knows your body inside and out. And the Great Physician knows the things that you need for your body to be healed, restored, and made perfectly whole.

What Happened in the Garden

In Genesis 3, we find that Eve took from the fruit and gave it to her husband. Verse 17 says, "And to Adam He (God) said, because you have listened to the voice of your wife, you have eaten of the tree of which I commanded you, you shall not eat of it. Cursed is the ground because of you. In toil you shall eat of it all the days of your life. Thorns and thistles it shall bring forth to you and you shall eat the plants of the field. And in the sweat of your face you shall eat bread until you return to the ground, for out of it you were taken. You are dust, and to dust you will return."

Did God say anything about sickness, illness, disease, toil or dying before the fall, and before sin came into the world? Not at all. But after the fall, things changed. The curse entered the earth. Sickness was introduced into the earth. These things did not originate with God and were not a part of the original creation. Rebellion to God's directions opened the door and brought sickness. Disobedience brought sickness and death into the world. The curse of the fall began to perpetuate in the earth.

So let me ask you a question: When did death come into the picture? After disobedience! Sin carried with it sickness and disease. Who brought it? Who brought sin and death, and sickness into the world? Was it God? No! Notice, through deception that led man into disobedience to God's instruction, the serpent, the enemy of your soul, the devil is the one that provoked the entrance of sickness into the earth. And he's used it as a tool, as a device and weapon of oppression against man, ever since.

Bound by Satan

In Luke 13, there was a synagogue ruler who was mad at Jesus. He was angered because Jesus had healed this woman who had been sick for 18 years. In fact, all the religious leaders were mad at Jesus for healing that woman. When you read the entire story, you can hear their pride and arrogance, and the reverence they had for their rules, rituals and traditions. They had seemingly little regard for the woman and didn't care that she had been freed from the severely cruel prison of her sickness of almost two decades. It's like they didn't care about people's needs being met as much as their traditions being preserved.

Jesus' response to them set the record straight about healing and the source of sickness. "Ought not this woman, a daughter of Abraham, whom Satan bound 18 years, be loosed from this bond on the Sabbath?" Wait, what? Who did Jesus say bound that lady? Jesus said it was Satan who bound and oppressed her with sickness for all that time. Jesus is a truth teller. Can He lie, or embellish and exaggerate the truth? Of course not! And here in Luke 13:16, Jesus says this woman was a daughter of Abraham, meaning she has legal and full covenant rights and privileges to be completely healed.

Jesus said she was bound by Satan, not by God. Being bound by Satan and freed by God are in contrast as two separate functions and experiences. God frees and liberates people. The enemy binds and oppresses people. Jesus went on to say that there should be no problem, not only with her being healed, but being healed on the Sabbath day. This mention of the Sabbath indicates that she wasn't healed on the basis of how perfect she was, how long she endured this infirmity, or on how much she learned from this sickness, but showed that healing was a provisional reality under covenant rights and the finished work of creation.

What Did Jesus Do When He Came?

Now that you understand where sickness came from it is important that you know what Jesus did when He came to this earth. Matthew 4:23 gives a clear description of an important aspect of Jesus' mission in the earth. Matthew 4:23 says, "And He went about all Galilee teaching in their synagogue, preaching the gospel of the Kingdom and healing every disease, and every infirmity among the people." Why would Jesus do that if He had put sickness on them? It wouldn't make any sense for Jesus to create the demand for healing by imposing a great supply of sickness.

It would be like your insurance agent walking out to your car at his office with his clipboard to evaluate the condition of your car. He starts looking to make sure that you don't have any hail damage, no previous body damage from prior accidents and he finishes his inspection to see that your car is in great shape. And then he walks over to his car, pops the trunk and pulls out a sledgehammer and just starts repeatedly beating your car and busting out the windshield and windows with this sledge hammer.

You would be confused. You've signed your policy for full coverage and the agent has now created the need for a damage claim to be filed that his company is going to have to pay for in full. The agent was both the destroyer and the restorer. You would have a puzzled look on your face and a sense of amazement at the stupidity of the agent. It doesn't make any kind of business sense, and operating like that he won't be in business long.

That's what it would be like to think that God put sickness on people. God does not put sickness on people to then just turn around and heal them. God is the Healer. That's who He is. He was good from the beginning. Remember – *good God; bad devil.* In the beginning when He first created everything that we see, and everything that we experience, He wanted all to be perfect. He wanted a perfect environment. He didn't create sickness and disease as part of that environment.

Who makes people sick? Think about it again. Jesus healed every disease and every infirmity among the people. "Healer" is who He is. Jesus heals the sick. Here's the truth that I want you to know and never forget. Think about it. Meditate on it. Write it down. Say it, talk about it, and pray in the confidence of this truth. John 10:10 says, "The thief comes only to steal, and to kill and destroy. But I came that they may have life…" This is Jesus talking about His role in the earth. And He goes on to say that He not only came to give life on every level, but life more abundantly.

In John 6:38, Jesus said He came not to do His own will, but the will of the Father who sent Him into the earth. Jesus also said that "if you've seen Me, you've seen the Father." In John 8:28-29, Jesus said, "…I do nothing of Myself, but as My Father taught Me, I speak these things…for I always do those things that please Him." What do all these things mean? It clearly explains that Jesus was the representative of God and His will in the earth. This presents Jesus as the expressed and manifested will of God in the earth for all men and for all time. It means that whatever you hear Jesus saying and see Jesus doing in the earth, it is definitively the will of God in the earth.

In John 10:10 Jesus wasn't just saying that he wants us to live, to be alive, have a heartbeat and live in the earth for a certain number of years. That's not all He was talking about. He used the word that relates to the Greek word "zoe" which means the "God-kind of life." What He means is He came so that you could live in such a way that you're victorious over every symptom or sickness that would try to come against your body. He means for healing to be yours on the basis of the atonement, and that the sacrifice of Jesus Christ and the stripes He bore on the way to the cross should take effect in your body to bring healing. The kind of life He was referring to, is a life perfected in the earth through the blood Jesus gave and the sin He forgave. Jesus was talking about a quality of life that maintains the divine spark of eternity while here in the earth, a life full of abundance, a life of blessing. That's what God wants for you, not for you to think that He put sickness on you.

We saw it there in the beginning, in Genesis, that God came creating life, not taking it! He came creating life in an environment where there was abundance to be enjoyed. What we need to understand, remember, and live by, is that Hebrews 13:8 says that Jesus Christ is the same yesterday, today and forever. What Jesus was doing when He walked the earth is the same thing He's doing today – healing the sick and all who are oppressed. He's still giving life and that more abundantly.

So if Jesus is the same yesterday, today and forever, and if God cannot lie, is no respecter of persons, and does not change, it makes no sense that God would heal people in Bible days and not heal people today. It makes no sense to think that Jesus healed before the resurrection, but after the resurrection He's making people sick, destroying people's lives with the ravages of disease, stealing husbands from wives, wives from husbands, parents from children and children from parents with sickness, illness, disease and death. If He's the same yesterday, today and forever, that means the same healing power that was available to those apostles, the disciples, and the people of that day, is ours today. The same power that raised Jesus from the dead is available to us today.

This same power worked through Peter and John when they were outside the Gate Beautiful and brought healing to a lame man with these words, "Silver and gold have I none, but in the name of Jesus, stand up and walk." This man had been lame from birth but in a moment of time, his feet and his ankle bones received strength and he got up and started walking and leaping and praising God. That same healing power is available to you everyday of your life to heal every sickness, and every disease. Why? Because we serve a great BIG God.

Your sickness is not bigger than God. God is bigger than your sickness. That's what you have to understand. That is the truth that will make you free to walk in health, wellness and victory. In talking about the devil, his wiles and weapons—which includes all those things that would make people sick and diseased—Colossians 2:15 tells us that "He disarmed principalities." He disarmed those principalities and powers and made a public example of them, triumphing over them in the cross of Jesus Christ.

When Jesus was nailed to the cross and with His arms stretched out wide, He said, "It is finished," The salvation of your soul and the spiritual right to be in heaven forever with Jesus was set in place for every man, woman, or child who would place their faith in Christ. When he said it's finished to acquire that salvation, with the atoning work of the blood of Christ, He also purchased our healing.

But it would be very difficult for you to get that healing if you don't think that God's bigger than your sickness. Sometimes we think things are big, but they're not so big when you have the right perspective and compare things with God. When something's standing right in front of the thing we need, it can block our sight making it hard to see anything past what's right in front of us. That's when we need to get a better perspective on things.

It's a Matter of Proximity

As a kid going on family vacations, I remember us driving to Colorado and looking out as we were riding on Highway 70 West. And when you're a ways off still in Oklahoma or Kansas, you don't see the Rocky Mountains. But finally after a while, way out in the distance you start to see something. It's small but you can tell that the landscape is changing. From a distance you don't realize how big those mountains are, but as you get closer and closer, that mountain begins to get bigger, and bigger, and bigger, until finally you get to the edge of the Rocky Mountains and you realize, "Those mountains are really big!"

I can remember being in Colorado once with my dad and I asked him, "Can we climb that mountain tomorrow?" And he was laughing. As a child, from a distance it looked like the mountains were like a hill. And it looked like it would take me about fifteen minutes to go to the top. But then you get closer to the mountains and you realize, "Wow, this is a lot bigger up close!"

Too many times what people do is get their sickness, disease, and the doctor's reports right in front of their faces and foremost in their minds. People go home from the doctor and investigate on the internet. They start looking up all the symptoms, side effects, and stages of a sickness, and make the case really big.

Runny nose. "Hey, my nose is running." Blurry vision. You were looking at the internet for twelve hours. "I do have blurry vision." Headaches. "I'm feeling a little headache coming on." Fever. "Honey, do I feel hot?"

People kind of laugh or nod their heads at this because we've all done it. The doctor's got his reports and charts and we're looking over his shoulder and start wondering what he's writing and how come he's not talking. We want to know what the doctor says instead of putting our faith in a risen

Savior and looking for what God says about our healing.

- *He says, "You're healed."*

- *He says, "I'm the Great Physician."*

- *He says, "Jesus bore your sicknesses and carried your pains."*

- *He says, "I've forgiven all your iniquities and healed all your diseases."*

- *He says, "You're redeemed from the curse of the law."*

- *He says, "I'm bigger than sickness and disease. I'm bigger than cancer. I'm bigger than heart disease. I don't care what runs in the family and all the other things that you might be worried about."*

You were bought with a price and He purchased your body. God made your body so that you could walk in complete victory and complete healing, and it can happen right now today. Do you believe in a BIG God? We're not to be supporters or receivers of sickness and disease. Let me reiterate an earlier point. I respect doctors and the long hours of sacrifice and commitment they have to their profession and to seeing people healed, but I don't place my ultimate faith in what the doctors do or don't say. They don't have the final authority. I can listen to what doctors say, honor, and thank them for their assistance, and as God leads, I can act on recommendations and remedies they prescribe. But the bottom line is, I place my faith in a BIG God who's bigger than any bad report or negative diagnosis a doctor may bring based on facts they learned from an exam and a textbook.

God has the final authority. He's bigger than what the tests have to say. I know that the vast majority of doctors are doing all they know to do to help heal the body, and that doctors are doing their jobs as professionals, but doctors aren't bigger than God. God is bigger than all the symptoms and reports that might be factual. I'm not saying they are to be ignored as if they don't exist. But the facts of a sickness aren't bigger than the truth of God. He's the Healer. He's a big God. He's bigger than all of that.

God Showed Up

In Africa, when I preached out in the villages where there were no doctors and there's no medical help coming, I told them that God was bigger than whatever problems they were facing. If God didn't heal them, they were going to stay sick. The Spirit of God would show up and with great conviction we would tell them, "God's bigger than HIV. God's bigger than AIDS. I don't care if the whole family has it, God is bigger than that."

We would see notable miracles and supernatural demonstrations because when people put their faith in God and just how big He really is, miracles happen. Believe this today. Believe what the scriptures have to say. This is how we get sickness out of the way, and get God right in front of our eyes, in our ears, and in the midst of our hearts and minds. God has to become bigger than sickness. That's what has to happen to see the bigness of God overtake the sickness.

We can't always be talking about the sickness as if it's greater than God. We can't spend much of our time talking about how sick we are instead of what God's word has to say about our sickness. When we do that, we're just rehearsing the sickness in our mind. God's bigger than a report of having only days, months, or weeks to live. Let your mind and words be stayed on Him, spend the bulk of your time talking about how BIG God is, and how great a Healer He is, and He'll keep you in perfect peace.

If we spend too much time talking and thinking about what others are saying about how bad it is, we're looking at the disease. If we're researching the disease on the internet to see pictures and testimonies about the disease, then it's going to make the size of the disease on your mind get bigger. If you're going to do anything with the internet, or books, or people, find out what worked for people who survived and lived. Find out about people who've made it – find out what they said, what they thought, how they looked to, and focused on God. Search the scriptures diligently for the answers that will put you over the top.

If you can't find something good on the internet then turn it off. And whatever else you might be doing to stay focused on your healing, open your Bible and stay attuned to what God said in His Word about healing and what He is saying in your heart about your healing. Open the word of God and see what God says about that disease. He says, "By Jesus' stripes you are healed." He says He's made a way for you to be well. He says you're redeemed from the curse of the law, including every type of sickness, illness, or disease. He says He wants you to be in health. He says He'll protect you, preserve you, and promote you into good health. He wants you to know how to walk in divine healing and divine health.

With that said, let me give you four ways to see healing take place in your life.

Four Things

Number one—Get closer to God than your sickness. Get

closer to God's way of thinking, and speaking, and acting, about healing. Let God's perspective of life over death and healing over sickness permeate your thoughts and days. James 4:7-8 says, "Submit yourselves therefore to God. Resist the devil and he will flee from you. Draw near to God and He will draw near to you."

Get closer to God than you are to your sickness by spending time looking at, reading, memorizing, speaking, and believing what God says about being healed. Listen for His voice to give you directions and instructions on how to practically apply what you're seeing in the scriptures. See yourself being well and living well. Understand that God is greater than the pain, the symptoms, the fears and the negative thoughts and pictures the enemy will try to show you. Ask God for the right thoughts to think, the right pictures to see within yourself and the best words that you can be speaking over your life and throughout your day.

There comes a time when you have to separate yourself from the voices and people that are influencing you more about sickness than God is influencing you about healing. People can be well-meaning to show care by bringing up how bad you've got it, or how bad you look or must feel, but at that moment they're not helping you. At that moment, you need to be closer to God than closer to people who may not be talking like God speaks in the Word. Draw near to God and He will draw near to you.

Number two. Believe that God wants to heal you. That's hard for people. It was hard for me many years, until after a while, I just saw so many people being healed of things that doctors said there's either no hope or they'll have this condition the rest of their lives. In Africa and other places around the world where there are no doctors, and they don't have doubt and unbelief to cloud their minds, they just get healed. Believe that God wants to heal you.

And if you need proof, write this down. Read Matthew 8. Read the whole thing. The leper in this story came to Jesus and said, "Lord, I've got this leprosy. If you're willing, you can heal me." And Jesus looked back at him as if to say, "Willing? What are you talking about? Willing?"

"I'm willing" is what the Bible tells us. One translation says, "Of course I'm willing!" It's always God's will to heal you. You have to get past the thought or fear that God's not willing to heal you. It is God's will for you to be healed. God didn't put sickness on you. He came to bring you life, and life more abundantly, not sickness and disease. Jesus didn't come into the earth to teach people a lesson by putting cancer on them. That's not what the Bible says. It's the Word of God which is the truth, and that will make you free!

Number three. Remove all doubt and unbelief. Look at Matthew 13:53-58.

> And it came to pass, that when Jesus had finished these parables, he departed thence. And when he was come into his own country, he taught them in their synagogue, insomuch that they were astonished, and said, Whence hath this man this wisdom, and these mighty works? Is not this the carpenter's son? Is not his mother called Mary? And his brethren, James, and Joses, and Simon, and Judas? And his sisters, are they not all with us? Whence then hath this man all these things? And they were offended in him. But Jesus said unto them, A prophet is not without honor, save in his own country, and in his own house. And he did not many mighty works there because of their unbelief.

Jesus was teaching in His hometown and in Matthew 13:58

the Bible says, "And He did not do many miracles there because of their lack of faith." He just didn't do it. Notice why – because of their unbelief. They refused to believe, they refused to be persuaded that God was bigger than anything and everything else connected to sickness. They shut Jesus out. They refused to have faith in Jesus to heal. They placed more faith in the sickness than they did in Jesus. That's called unbelief.

When belief is misplaced and focused against God this hinders a person from receiving what is promised by God. God operates through faith, but it's faith *in Him*.

And that's **Number four.** God moves through faith. Faith is a legal invitation for God to get involved in our lives and address our needs. He understands our needs and has compassion towards us, but He's not moved by needs alone. Multitudes of people have needs all over the world. God is aware and sensitive to your need, but He's moved through faith.

In Matthew 17:20, the disciples couldn't heal a boy being affected by epilepsy. The Bible says he was tormented by a spirit, not that he was tormented by God. He was tormented by a spirit that opposed God and oppressed the boy. The disciples came to Him and said, "Lord, why couldn't we heal this boy?" And Jesus said, "Because of your little faith. For truly I say unto you, if you have faith as a grain of mustard seed, you will say to this mountain, move from here to there, and it will move, and nothing will be impossible to you."

What will be impossible to you if you have faith as a grain of mustard seed? Nothing. Can you slip something that's impossible to God into the equation? No. If you have faith, nothing will be impossible for you, because we have access to the greatest and most powerful Person in the entire universe—this great, BIG God.

How about the promise found in Mark 11:24?

Therefore I tell you, whatever you ask for in prayer, believe that you receive it and it will be yours. And whenever you stand praying, forgive if you have anything against anyone, so that your Father also who is in heaven may forgive you your trespasses.

Forgiveness

So there are two keys here. If we're to understand that God moves through faith, we have to understand these two things. The first thing is that you must believe that you received the object of your prayer when you prayed. Number two is, don't come expecting healing from God when you haven't forgiven somebody that you're holding bitterness against. Faith toward God requires a heart that's confident toward God. Holding unforgiveness will cause your heart to shrink away from God and lack confidence toward Him. If you're holding onto unforgiveness, that's the bad news. The good news is that you can forgive in a moment's time. You can decide to forgive someone immediately.

If somebody were to ask me what's the one thing that keeps people from being healed, I would say they have unforgiveness in their heart toward some other person. A pastor, a church, or the people they work with, their neighbor, a spouse, parent, child, or other family member has hurt and offended them. Whatever the reason, people can have unforgiveness and hold onto and not have the capacity for their heart to fill up with healing because it's filled with unforgiveness.

Unforgiveness in your heart can hinder you from being healed. Believe you receive healing and forgive others. You can do both right now, wherever you are. You don't have to wait to get to church; you don't have to call someone for prayer. You can believe you receive right now, and you can forgive right now. When you do this, you will push the hang-ups about healing out of the picture and you'll invite this BIG God to do BIG things in healing your body. The Word of God is the truth – not what's happened to you in the past. God is bigger. God is bigger than any of the injustices, hurts, rejections, or offenses in your life. You can make the decision to believe you receive and forgive right now.

The Bible also says in James 5, "Is any among you sick? Let him call for the elders of the church and let them pray over him, anointing them with oil in the name of the Lord. And the prayer of faith will save the sick man and the Lord will raise him up, as if he has committed no sin. He will be forgiven."

There are times when you need the help of others to stand in faith for your healing, and that's ok, too. You can call for, or call on, the elders of the church, and they can pray for you by faith, believing that God's word is true and takes precedence over any bad reports. The reports contain limited knowledge. But God is unlimited. He's able to do more than you could ever ask or think.

If you've had a condition for a long time, remember the woman who got healed of a spirit of infirmity after 18 years, and the man lame from birth who got healed from his long-standing crippled condition. If you've heard the report saying your condition isn't curable, remember that the Bible says things that are impossible with man are possible with God. Nothing is too difficult for the Lord and all things are possible with Him.

Decide today, right now, to be healed. Decide to believe God. Decide to believe the good report of the scriptures. Stand in faith on the Word of God, believe God for healing and speak the Word of healing into your life. Forgive anyone you need to forgive. It doesn't matter how long you've had a condition or who's saying it's not possible to be well. God is bigger than the obstacles you might face. God is bigger than the problems related to your condition. He's bigger than the sickness.

God loves you and is concerned about you. He purchased healing for you so that you could be well and whole. Now is the time to speak your faith and let words of life, health and strength flood your life. If you're ready to let God be bigger than sickness of any kind speak these words out loud:

> *God is BIGGER than my problem. God is BIG-*
> *GER than my sickness. God is BIGGER than*
> *my fears. I'm ready to receive healing in my body*
> *from my great, BIG, enormous God. He's BIG-*
> *GER than my problems, He's BIGGER than*
> *my sickness and disease, and He's BIGGER than*

anything I could ever face.

"Lord Jesus, wherever I've sinned against Your Word, I ask Your forgiveness. Lord, forgive me for my trespasses and forgive me for my sins. Lord Jesus, just as You are forgiving me now, I forgive every person who has ever hurt me. I forgive freely any who have done me wrong. You know their names, and You know what's happened, and today, Lord, through Your power, I forgive them. I release it to You, God. I release any unforgiveness in my life, and I stand upon Your Word right now for complete healing in my body. And I forgive myself for not believing in how BIG You are God. I believe Jesus is my Healer. And I believe You are my BIG God who's BIGGER than all.

Chapter Six: God Is Bigger Than Your Money

Do You Hate Money?

"I hate money!" How many times have you ever heard that statement? How many times have you said it yourself? If you've ever wanted something really bad or got yourself in a bind because you overextended your resources, you know what I'm talking about. Before my wife and I understood God's heart concerning money, and what He wants to do in our finances, we had a lot of conversations that ended with, "I hate money."

And usually these conversations happen about the time bills are due. If you're like I once was, as long as there was enough to cover the bills each week, I did not concern myself about money. However, when there was not enough, I stressed out. This tension wreaked havoc on my relationship with my wife, children, and all those around me. Looking back, it is strange to think that a piece of paper dyed green could have that much control over me.

As much as we may not like it, money can cause us to have some kind of negative emotion one way or another. It's just a piece of paper that's supposed to represent some gold or financial substance somewhere. But if not managed, understood, or regarded in proper perspective, money can cause a lot of heartache and stress. For that reason, we must learn the principles necessary to be the master over what God has given us. God never intended for money (or the lack thereof) to dictate our emotions and ultimately our happiness.

This is especially true for the believer. I can understand how those who are not applying Godly principles to their finances could get into financial trouble. In fact, the person who is not applying ANY principles to their finances is in trouble already! I know unbelievers who are living from paycheck to paycheck and barely getting by. I see them scraping and saving and struggling just to survive from day to day. I feel for them because they don't have the hand of God protecting their money. However, for the believer it is not the destiny

God desires or designs for us. It's not what's supposed to be happening for the believer. It breaks my heart when a believer comes to me in financial ruin because they failed to apply the principles God has given us in His Word.

As believers we have the provision of God upon our lives. I don't believe that we're supposed to be just barely getting by. This belief is not based on a "wish," it's based on the scriptures. The Bible is clear. The believer should not be living paycheck to paycheck. God has limitless resources. He doesn't want to withhold things from us. He doesn't want to bar us from things that would allow us to get ahead. God wants the best for you and me because He loves us!

What Does God Want?

Does God want to keep us in poverty? Is it God's will that we stay in poverty worrying about bills all the time? Do you think God is pleased with families in turmoil over money? Do you think He wants married couples fighting with one another about money, and telling their kids *no* to everything because there's no extra money?

Or could it be, that He who gives power to create and obtain wealth, is willing to funnel some of that money into the hands of those that are completely committed to Him? God wants to do more than just provide for your needs. God is a God of abundance. You have to ask yourself, "Would it be fine with Him, that I actually lived in abundance?" We must move past this thinking that our loving heavenly Father would keep us in poverty.

You are an Heir

Some people call this kind of thinking crazy. But before you tune me out, understand I'm not talking about unbalanced and unscriptural teaching on prosperity. I'm not saying that God wants everybody to live in a 15,000 square foot house, have ten cars, four boats, two bars of gold, and never have to work again. That's not what I'm saying at all. What I am saying to you is that God is BIG enough to provide for all of your needs, but He is also able to provide above and beyond your needs so that your life can be a testimony of how a believer is to live! After all, are you not an heir? Are you not part of a kingdom where the King has unlimited resources?

God will meet all of our needs, but is it really possible that He wants to actually take us from just having our needs covered to living in abundance? Yes! God is bigger than our financial and material needs. God is not just a resource for living, but also the Source for *all* things. God is bigger than your money woes. He's bigger than your paycheck. He's bigger than your retirement account. He's bigger than your 401k. He's bigger than anything financial in your life. God is bigger than your finances! You should just yell that out loud right now. (Unless you're in a crowded coffee shop).

But in order to experience our financial needs being met, and living in His abundance, there are some things with which we have to deal. What kind of a testimony is it for a child of God to be barely getting by when we serve a great, BIG, awesome God? How can we sit and look at our children in the face and say, "God is a God who will bless you financially," if all they really see is an example of living from financial hardship to financial hardship. It's hard to sell that to our children especially when they get older and understand more.

By now, I pray that you are asking yourself, "Could it be that God really wants me to live in abundance? If so, what am I missing?" If the scripture is true (and trust me it is), but you're not seeing this kind of blessing, then maybe there's something missing in your Christian walk. Could it be possible that something is not allowing you to live in that abundance? Could it be that there's a hindrance that's keeping you in that "paycheck-to-paycheck" prison? Maybe there's something that's pulling you down or causing you to barely keep your head above water.

A God of Abundance

There came a time in my Christian life, as I read and studied the Word, that God began to reveal Himself to me as a God of abundance. To me, it looked like God wanted to provide, not just for my needs, but He wanted to give me *more than enough*. As I searched the scriptures, I saw that God wanted to meet all our needs, but also wanted us to have enough to give away to help other people. As I searched the scriptures, I became highly motivated to do more than just barely keep my head above water. I wanted to be able to give more to missionaries, more to my church, more to those in need. But, how was I going to do those things if I couldn't even pay the electric bill?

The more I studied about this, the more I realized we serve the God who owns it all, and it would not make sense that His desire would be to keep us one dollar above poverty. This kind of thinking can be a stretch for our minds, because what has been taught in many circles for many years, is that God wants to keep us down to keep us humble. But what I want you to understand is that when you are faithful with little tiny things, God sees that He can trust you. And when we prove ourselves faithful and trustworthy, He'll allow you to have more. It is not a "God issue" that keeps us in poverty, it's an "*us issue*"!

Too often it's our mind problem that prevents us from having more than enough. Maybe sometimes we feel guilty if we have a little more. We'll see somebody less fortunate than us and perhaps feel self conscious about being blessed. But it's always been God's idea and plan to see His creation, His family, well taken care of and provided for in every circumstance and season of life. In order to experience it, I think there are three things that we need to understand about God, so that He can truly become bigger than our money.

It's all His anyway

If I have a one hundred dollar bill and send my son to the grocery store with a list of things that he is supposed to get with that hundred dollar bill, the second he leaves the house, does this money become his money? Or is it still my money? It's still my money! (He might not say that though.) Regardless of what he does with it, whether he obeys or disobeys with what I tell him, this IS my money.

The first thing that I want you to understand is that it is all God's anyway. Ultimately, every penny we have, every ounce of our material possessions, every dollar in our bank accounts, every asset connected with our 401k and IRA is His. He gave us the favor, wisdom, strength, opportunity, and direction necessary to acquire the wealth in our possession. What you have, to any degree, comes from God.

Psalm 24:1 says, "The earth is the Lord's and the fullness thereof, the world and those who dwell therein." It is all God's. However, we don't want to believe that, do we? That's hard for us sometimes. We don't want it to be God's. We want it to be ours. We think about how hard we've worked, and all the sacrifices we've made, and we believe those things brought us what we have.

While those are good traits to have, no matter how you slice it or dice it, it all comes from God. After you move it around from account to account, after you buy and sell your stocks, after you invest in or sell your business, it is all His anyway.

In Matthew 25, Jesus told a story we call the Parable of Talents. This story illustrates what I'm talking about.

"For it will be as when a man going on a journey called his servants and entrusted to them his property." (*Whose property was it? It was the property of the property owner.*) "To one he gave five talents, to another two, to another one; to each according to his ability. Then he went away. He who had received the five talents went at once and traded with them, and he made five talents more. So also, he who had two talents made two more talents. But he who had received just the one talent went and dug in the ground and hid his Master's money." I'll pause the story here to ask you again, whose money was it? It was still the Master's money!

The story continues, "Now after a long time the Master of those servants came and settled accounts with them. And he who had received the five talents came forward, bringing five talents more, saying, Master, you delivered to me five talents. Here I have made five talents more." Listen to what the Master says. "His Master said to him, Well done, good and faithful servant. You have been faithful over little. I will set you over much. Enter into the joy with your Master."

The man with the two talents came forward saying, "Master, you delivered to me two talents. Here I have made two talents more." His Master said to him, "Well done, good and faithful servant. You have been faithful over little, I will make you ruler over much. Enter into the joy of your Master."

Did you notice something strikingly similar between these first two servants? They realized that it was not their money. They worked their business and conducted their lives with respect to the fact that they were dealing with the Master's money. They didn't go into town and start wasting their Master's money or squandering their time on fruitless endeavors. They realized whose money they were holding. They were conscious at all times that they were holding the Master's money and that the Master was going to ask them to give an accounting for what they did with it. They knew he was going to return one day, and he was going to ask them, "What did you do with my money?"

Verse 24 goes on to say, "He also, who had received the one talent came forward saying, "Master..." (*Notice, he called him "Master," but did he actually believe He truly was?*) He said, "Master, I knew you to be a hard man, reaping where you did not sow, and gathering where you did not winnow. So I was afraid, and I went and hid the talent in the ground. Here, you have what is yours."

But his Master answered him, "You wicked and slothful servant." See what happened here? The Master called him lazy. To those first two he said, "Thank you for doing something with my money." With that last one he said, "You did nothing? You're lazy!" He called him wicked and slothful. "You say that I reap where I have not sowed and gather where I have not winnowed?"

The tone in the Master's voice was, "What do you mean you knew that I reap where I have not sown, and gather where I have not winnowed?" It was almost like he was saying to this servant, "You call me Master, but you don't know me at all. You couldn't know me if you think that I'm the kind of Master that would reap in places I have not sown or gather in places I did not winnow. You're calling me deceitful."

Basically the Master is saying to this last servant, "You don't know me at all. These other two servants, they know me. They know that I gave them a little bit and tested them with it, and then at the end of the day I said come on, let's all enjoy it together. But you, you went and hid it. You don't know me. You don't know me at all!"

Let's finish out the story in verse 27. The Master said to the one with one talent, "You ought to have invested my money with the bankers and at my coming I should have received what was mine with interest. So take the talent from him and give it to the one who has ten talents. For to everyone who has will more be given, and he will have abundance."

That's a pretty incredible statement. To everyone who has more will be given, and he will have abundance. But from him who has not, even what he has will be taken away. And matters grew even worse for the servant with one talent when the Master said, "Cast this worthless servant into the outer darkness where there will be weeping and gnashing of teeth."

Those first two servants understood that this was the Master's money. It was not their money. And they truly knew the Master. They truly knew that if he said, "I'm coming back," he meant, "I'm coming back."

The talents being referred to in this story represents money. They knew that when they were handed the talents, they received them knowing that the Master did not give those talents to them just to spend it on their own good pleasure. They knew that the money belonged to the Master, that he was coming back and he was expecting them to have caused it to grow. They knew the Master. They knew that he was a man of his word.

The third servant didn't know his Master. It's important we don't adopt the attitude or actions of this third servant. He was called wicked for doing nothing with the money that was given to him. He simply did the easiest thing he could do. Bury it, and forget about it. You always get nothing out of nothing. He made excuses. He only *thought* he knew the Master.

There's something else to notice here. You can see how the first two servants worked to grow the Masters money,

THEN they enjoyed the abundance *with* the Master. Many people flip this principle around. They spend the money that God is testing them with on things that do not bring increase. Thus, failing the test and ending up like the lazy servant in the story.

This third servant's beliefs seemed acceptable, but the principle of the story tells us differently. The money belonged to the Master, but he didn't give it to him for safekeeping. He gave the talent to this servant for him to cause it to grow and increase. He gave it to him in order for it to grow and become greater than where it started. What we're given doesn't affect just us. If it were just us that it was going to affect, it wouldn't matter. What you do with what you're given affects others in a great way.

This was the Master's money; this was the money test. He was testing these servants to see if they could be faithful with just a little bit. Why do you think he did that? Because next time he goes on a journey, he wants to give them more. He wants to give them abundance. Because if they're faithful in little, then the Master knows they will be faithful with everything.

In our case, this is where the Master really gets to see if we can handle a real blessing. Notice he didn't start them with abundance. He basically gave them what they needed to get started. Some went out and they did what they were supposed to do with it.

Obviously you've made the connection by now; it is not just a story about servants. It's a story that illustrates how the money that we have belongs to God. And if the money that we have belongs to God, then it's very important that we find out what we're supposed to do with it.

What Are We to do With the Master's Money?

It's extremely important what you do with the Master's money, because He's watching. He wants to see if you'll be faithful with the little bit that he's given you. So, where does that begin?

First, give the tithe. My wife and I give ten percent back into the work of the kingdom. God will never be bigger than your money until you give the tithe. When you do not tithe, God is looking and saying, "I meet your needs but you're not really being faithful with that little tiny bit that I've given you. I want to give you more but I cannot even trust you with that ten percent. So why would I ever move you past need and into abundance?"

Malachi 3:8-11 says:

Will a man rob God? Yet you are robbing Me! But you say, "How have we robbed You?" In tithes and offerings. "You are cursed with a curse, for you are robbing Me, the whole nation of you! "Bring the whole tithe into the storehouse, so that there may be food in My house, and test Me now in this," says the LORD of hosts, "if I will not open for you the windows of heaven and pour out for you a blessing until it overflows. "Then I will rebuke the devourer for you, so that it will not destroy the fruits of the ground; nor will your vine in the field cast its grapes," says the LORD of hosts.

Never Met a Broke Tither

There are several truths that I know about finances. I've never in my life met a broke tither. I've never met somebody that tithed and was only able to eat one meal a day or starving. Even in my times living in Africa I noticed those that lived in grass huts in remote villages, would tithe something. If they didn't even operate off the money system, they tithed their food. I've seen villagers bring bananas for their tithe.

I'll repeat it again, I have never met a broke tither.

And do you know why? It's because God honors those who are obedient to His Word. I think that failure to abide by this principle keeps more people from living in abundance than any other. Because of this, it's very difficult for people to move from barely getting by to living in God's abundance.

Know Where Your Money Goes

Secondly, you need to know where you're money is going. It's amazing to me how many people I counsel that have money trouble and do not know where their money is going each month. You cannot be a "good and faithful servant" if you don't know what's happening with the Master's money! It seems to be a commonality for those in money trouble. Money comes in and goes out, but little is done to monitor and evaluate how the money is being used as a whole. They don't have a budget. They have no idea where the money is going each week. They act as though something strange has happened. "It's like I got paid and poof it was gone!" The money went, and they failed to pay attention to how it was spent. You have to know where it is going.

Eliminate Debt

Next, you need to work on eliminating your debt. You can't just pay the minimum on your credit cards, month after month, or else it'll take you 30 years to pay it off. Proverbs 22:7 says, "The rich rules over the poor, and the borrower is slave to the lender." I don't want to be a slave to anybody. Do you?

Even if you're paying a small amount over the minimum payment, do it! Something that worked for our family when we were pulling out of debt – make a list of all your liabilities (fancy word for debt owed), then target your smallest amount. Attack it like a pit bull! Write down the payments you're putting toward it, making sure to adjust the balance. It will become fun to watch it go down. There is a caveat to this however. You and your spouse must be doing this together. It will make no sense for one to be attacking debt and another spending.

Open a Savings Account

Finally, open a savings account. Save some of the Master's money. Do something with it. Save it. Put a little bit in from every paycheck. My grandfather use to say, "If you can only save a nickel, every paycheck, save a nickel." I would rather be faithful with that nickel, than just to say, "Well, I don't have enough to save." I promise you, you can save something if you get in the habit of saving.

Proverbs 13:22 says, "A good man leaves an inheritance to his children's children; but the sinners wealth is stored up for the righteous." We should be setting aside money, not only for our children but also for our grandchildren. Can you imagine how different your life would be if your grandparents, from the very first moment that they ever received a paycheck, began to put money to the side for your kids? By now, there would be quite a bit of money in there. It is never too late to start! You can start saving right now for your grandchildren. What would happen if a whole group of people began to do that? You know what we would have? We would have blessed children!

God Takes Care of Your Needs

I want you to understand that God will take care of your needs because you are His child. Let's go back to the example I spoke of earlier about giving my son money for groceries. If I take that hundred dollars and I give it to me son, saying "Go in the store, and I want you to get eggs, milk, bread and meat. Then I want you to meet me back here at the car."

When I send him into the grocery store, it's important what he does with that money because it's not his money. If he comes back with video games, candy, and baseball cards, did he do what he was told by the one who gave him the money?

What possible reason could he give me that would make me think he did what I told him to do with the money? If I send someone to make purchases on my behalf and give them very specific instructions of what to do with the money, and if that person violated my trust, first of all I would not be pleased – secondly, I could not be quick to trust them with more money in the future.

Now if my son returns and didn't do what I told him to do with this money, should I cut off all the food from him? Would I be justified to stop supplying for his basic needs as my child? Would you do that? Would you tell your child:

> *"I sent you after meat, eggs, potatoes and you came*
> *back with video games? That's it! You're kicked*
> *out of the family! You don't get to eat at the table.*
> *Matter of fact, you better stay out of my refrigera-*
> *tor. That's all mine in there."*

No good parent would make their child suffer to the point of starving them or putting them out of the house for misusing money on this level. We wouldn't do that and God won't do it either. This demonstrates the level of grace God gives to us.

Need versus Blessing

To some, what I'm saying here may sound controversial. However the fact is that God will still meet your basic needs if you don't tithe, because He loves you, and because He's your Father. The Word says, "The Lord is my Shepherd. I shall not be in want." It also says, "I've been young, and now I'm old, and yet I've never seen the righteous forsaken, nor his seed begging bread." Because He's your Father, He will take care of you.

If God banished us out of the kingdom every time we disobeyed, if He locked the door to the refrigerator and left us in poverty at every misstep we made over the course of a lifetime, none of us would survive. I'm not saying we should resign ourselves to live lives of disobedience, but if God was going to shut us out every time that we disobeyed, we would all be in poverty, without food, shelter or any of our basic needs being covered.

When I say that God is a loving Father who will still meet our basic needs if we don't tithe, I'm not promoting some new doctrine or presenting a new theological twist. I'm saying that God is a good God, a perfect Father, and He cares about His children. Basic needs are food, water, shelter and clothing. He meets our need because He loves us.

Philippians 4:19 says, "And my God will supply every need of yours according to His riches in glory." That word "need" in the Greek is the word "chreia." It means, "necessity." It means, "I will supply every necessity – not video games." God promises to give us food, water, shelter, and clothing because He's our Father.

This word, "chreia," is used 49 times in the New Testament. It's found in Matthew 6:8, when Jesus was teaching us the importance of not being like the hypocrites and how they pray. He said, "Do not be like them (the hypocrites), for your Father knows what you have need of before you ask Him." He knows your necessity before you ask it.

Let me show you another example. We find it in Mark 2:25. The religious people were arguing about Jesus' disciples picking the heads off the grain and eating them on the Sabbath day. The religious people pointed fingers at what Jesus' disciples were doing. Jesus said, "Have you not ever read what David did when he was in need (chreia) and was hungry, he and those with him." They ate the showbread, the bread that was there on the altar. They ate it because they had a need. And God supplied their need with that showbread. It's a necessity—it's "chreia."

So you can see that because you are a child of God,

He will provide your "chreia," your necessity. He's not going to make you beg for bread, because the Lord is your Shepherd. You shall not want.

Stuck at *Necessity*

Now, why did I go into such detail about God meeting your necessity? It's because most believers are stuck at necessity, and they're completely satisfied with it. God's taking care of their need and that's enough for them.

Why is it that people will not trust God with ten percent of what He has already given them? Why is it that people won't tithe? I'll tell you why – because they're completely satisfied with just living in necessity. The sad fact is, living in necessity doesn't take any sacrifice at all.

Consider those people, who don't tithe, or haven't tithed for a very long time. Did they still eat? Did they still have clothing and a roof overhead? Sure they did! They may have been living paycheck to paycheck and barely getting by, but they had the necessities to survive. Is it possible that maybe God wants all of us to live on more than what it takes to barely get by? Unfortunately, most people are satisfied with chreia, and not taking part in and enjoying all of the kingdom benefits that are theirs. Things change when we move into full obedience.

Matthew 6:33 says, "Seek first His kingdom, and His righteousness, and all of these things will be added to you." When we put God, His kingdom and His righteousness first, (and keep Him there) God promises to add to us all the things we need. Continued obedience will move us into abundance.

Blessing

Let me show you another word – *blessing*. The word "blessing" means "above the basic need." Not just necessity, but above and more than enough. Blessing comes out of extreme obedience to what God's Word says.

Hebrews 11:6 says, "He's a rewarder to those who diligently seek Him." God is a rewarder. What does He reward them with? Just barely getting by? If He's a rewarder to those who diligently seek Him, does that just mean that He's going to only give you necessities? Rewarder doesn't really sound like a word that means "I'm just going to allow you to live paycheck to paycheck and have your needs met." It sounds much bigger than that.

There's a word in the Old Testament for blessing, and it's "beraka." So we have two words to remember:

- *"Chreia" which is need*

- *"Beraka" which is blessing*

Beraka means "prosperity, abundance and more than enough." The question you should be asking by now is, "How do I move from living in necessity to living in blessing." Or, "How do I move from living in chreia to living in baracha?"

The word "beraka" is found in Proverbs 10:22 which says, "The blessing of the Lord makes rich and adds no sorrow." Remember, we said that word blessing is "beraka" which means prosperity. So you can say, "The prosperity of the Lord makes rich and adds no sorrow in it." The blessing that's talked about is not limited to money, but definitely includes money. "The blessing of the Lord makes rich..."

I Samuel 30 is another place "beraka" is used. That's when David had recovered families and treasures that had been taken from him and his men by a band of Amalekites at Ziklag. After they had recovered all that was lost and took an abundance of extra goods from the Amalekites, he sent part of the spoil, or treasures, to his friends. They had abundance and they sent it to their friends, the elders of Judah, saying, "Here is a present for you from the spoil of the enemies of the Lord."

Now does that sound like David took what they needed to survive and gave it to those people, or that he gave out of his abundance? That's right, he gave out of their abundance!

What I want you to understand is that "beraka" means "above your basic needs." And God does that because He wants you to be a blessing to other people!

What kind of blessings are we talking about? One of the clearest explanations we can find of the blessings of the Lord is found in Deuteronomy 28. Beginning with verse 1 it says:

> *And if you obey the voice of the Lord your God, being careful to do all His commands which I command you this day, the Lord your God will set you on high above all the nations of the earth, and all these blessings shall come upon you and overtake you.*

Does that sound like He's going to meet just your basic need? Does God use terminology like, "These blessings are going to come upon you, they're going to track you down and overtake you so I can barely meet your basic need?" That doesn't sound right, does it? It sounds like to me that God's saying that something is going to be so BIG that it's going to exceed your basic needs and burst over into abundance and more than enough.

He goes on to say, "These blessings will overtake you if you obey the voice of the Lord your God." Remember, "beraka" means blessed, which means prosperity and abundance. So literally, you could use the word "prosperous" where you see the word "blessed" here in Deuteronomy 28.

Verse three then says,

Prosperous shall you be in the city, and prosperous shall you be in the field. Prosperous shall you be in the fruit of your body and the fruit of your ground, and the fruit of your beasts, and in the increase of your cattle, and in the young of your flock. Prosperous shall you be in the basket of your kneading trough. Prosperous shall you be when you come in, and prosperous shall you be when you go out. The Lord will cause your enemies to rise up against you and be defeated before you. They shall come out against you one way, and flee before you seven ways. The Lord will command His prosperity upon you, in your barns and in all that you undertake, and He will prosper you in the land which the Lord God gives you.

This doesn't sound like He's just talking about barely getting by. It doesn't sound like He's talking about only meeting your needs and giving you a dollar, dime, or nickel above poverty. This sounds like something much more. This sounds like abundance and more than enough.

Deuteronomy 28 goes on to say, "The Lord will establish you as a people holy to Himself. He has sworn to you, if you keep the commandments of the Lord your God, and walk in His ways, all the peoples of the earth shall see you are called by the name of the Lord, and they shall be afraid of you." Why? People will be afraid of you because you're blessed of the Lord. People will be afraid of you because you've got more than enough through the blessing of the Lord. People will be afraid of you because you are a child of God, you've got your needs met, you have abundance and because you're obedient to the Word of God. He brings abundance into your life and people will see that the hand of God is on your life. When you follow Him and heed His voice and His commandments, everything you touch prospers, and the spirit of abundance on your life touches everything that you lay your hand to. People will say, "Wow! Better pay attention to this person. God's hand is upon their life." And it only comes out of extreme obedience.

Verses 11 - 14:

And the Lord will make you abound in prosperity, in the fruit of your body, in the fruit of your cattle, in the fruit of your ground, within the land

which the Lord swore to your fathers to give you.
The Lord will open up to you His good treasury of
the heavens. The good treasury of heaven will be
opened to you to give you the rain of the land in
its season and bless all of the work of your hands.
And you shall lend to many nations, but you shall
not borrow. And the Lord will make you the head
and not the tail. You shall tend upward only, and
not downward; if you obey the commands of the
Lord your God which I command you this day,
being careful to do them.

How do we move into that blessing, into that "beraka" blessing, into that abundance blessing? You do it by obeying the
voice of the Lord. Many believers don't live in full obedience.
And you know what will happen to them? They'll get their
needs met. They'll live in necessity. But then there's this other
group of people that want God to be so pleased with them
that they're willing to obey and do everything that God has
asked them to do with everything in their life, including their
money.

And when God sees that, He says, "There is a servant
that's been faithful with little, I can make them rulers over
much. Let's go ahead and just bump them on over into beraka.

Let's go ahead and move them from chreia, from just barely seeing their needs being met, and let's move them over into abundance."

That's the person God doesn't have to worry about getting selfish. That's the person that will do with the Master's talents what the Master directs and expects. That's the person that proves themselves with the little amount God gives them, then God moves them over into abundance. Is that place of abundance the place in which you desire to live? At one time or another, we've all missed God's directions and were glad for seeing our necessities met. But there's a level of living that exceeds necessities that God has reserved for His child that determines to hear His voice and heed His commandments. God wants you blessed with abundance so you can be a blessing to others out of that abundance.

Test the Lord

When you get a revelation of what can happen for the faithful tither, it will radically change your life. You fully understand that there are windows of heaven that are strategically positioned to pour out blessings of abundance into your life. And the greatest part is that you won't have room enough to contain it all!

Still don't believe me? Fine, make it a test then. In fact, God said to test Him on it. Let me remind you again of our passage in Malachi 3:10 which say's, "Bring the full tithe into the storehouse that there may be food in my house, and thereby put Me to the test, says the Lord of hosts. If I will not open the windows of heaven for you and pour out for you an overflowing blessing. I will rebuke the devourer for you, so that it will not destroy the fruits of your soil, and your vine in the field shall not fail to bear, says the Lord of hosts. Then all of the nations shall call you blessed…" Or prosperous, or having an abundance…all of the nations will do that according to God. "For you will be a land of delight, says the Lord of hosts."

The Bible just said to go ahead and test the Lord. Basically, God said, "Test Me. Trust Me and see what I will do for you if you'll just be obedient to the tithe." If God were saying that He was only going to take care of your needs, would He say "overflowing"?

So the question really is, if you want God to be BIG in your finances, if you want God to be bigger than your money, what does it take? Quite honestly, it begins with you being obedient in your tithe. It takes being thankful that the Lord is giving you your "chreia," (need) but also knowing God wants you to live in "beraka" (blessed). God wants you to live in abundance, not just for the sake of selfishly living in abundance, but so that you can help more and more people, and draw more and more people to Him.

How exciting would it be to write a check and rebuild someone's house that got destroyed in a tornado, fire, or flood? What if you could write a check for $150,000, to build a widow lady a new house? What if you could wire the funds to supply fresh water wells to a region of villages in India or Africa? If you had the resources, would you build an orphanage to meet the "chreia" of homeless children? Would you feed families forced out of their homes because of civil war?

Do you think God wants you to do that? It doesn't make any sense that God wants us to be in poverty, so that we can't really help people. God wants us to live in abundance, so we can take that abundance and help people.

There are missionaries all over the world that are standing in front of people who have never heard the Gospel, not even one time. And that missionary stands in front of those people and declares that Jesus Christ came in the flesh, died on a cross and was raised from the dead. And these missionaries can't get there without money.

I've Been the Missionary

I'm passionate about this because I've been that missionary. I've personally seen the faces of people who are being changed by the message of Christ. And I've looked right into the face of other missionaries who had vision to change villages, cities, and nations but lacked the resources. If I could have been the one to write a $150,000 check, their lives and the lives of countless others could have been changed.

But I have also been the one that received the blessing. I know how to live in beraka, too. I was sitting at an airport in Rwanda years ago. As I was waiting for my plane to take off in the little coffee shop, I began to quietly pray to myself, "Lord, we sure could use the money to build this Life Center. You know our heart to get these ladies a place to learn English, and to learn the things that will help them get work and take care of their families."

These ladies were all infected with AIDS from being raped during the Rwandan genocide and we had a desire to help them, but simply didn't have the money. Right around the time I was praying, a doctor and his wife came into the coffee shop and sat right across from me. We began to talk since we were the only Americans in the airport. Soon, the doctor asked me what I was doing in Rwanda. I explained that my family and I served as Missionaries.

Then he asked me, "What are your biggest plans?"

I told him, "We want to build a Life Center and get these ladies who are suffering from AIDS into this place, and teach them how to work and supply for their families."

After a few minutes of conversation I got up to go to the restroom. When I came back that doctor looked over at me and he said, "My wife and I want to do something. We want to do something to help you get that building, to be able to put that Life Center in."

I gave him a card, and thanked him for his heart to help. Quite honestly, we've had many times that people offered to help us with the work of the ministry God's called us to, but over time, you learn that not everybody follows up on their good intentions. I didn't make any assumptions that we would ever hear from the doctor and his wife again.

Through it all God's been faithful. And at that point, my wife and I had been working hard in the ministry and tithing for years. You don't always know when that blessing is going to come. You just keep tithing and sowing, and tithing and sowing, tithing and sowing. I didn't know then, but in just a matter of days, the blessing would show up.

After that conversation, I boarded my flight and finally

arrived in Kenya. As I checked my email two days later, I was astounded at what I read. There in my inbox was an email from this doctor, which read, "My wife and I want to help you with this Life Center project. We're going to send you $50,000." Within two weeks the check arrived. Do you know what that was? That was the "beraka" blessing. I want to live there. What about you?

Chapter Seven: The BIG God of Your Future

Straying from God's Plan

God has always had BIG plans for man. It all started with the Creation and further unfolded when God blessed man with the charge to have dominion in the earth. He still wants man to display His dominion in the earth. God hasn't changed His mind about man as a race, nor you as an individual. He hasn't changed His mind about your present, nor your future. He felt the same way about Israel.

In Judges 6, after being wanderers in the desert, Israel was learning to live in the Promised Land, in all of the wealth and victory that God had brought them. They were settling into villages and putting down roots for the first time in their lives. They were working their own land, marrying, raising children, and building communities.

But something happened to the children of Israel early on. Despite the miracles and provision He had given them, they had forgotten the BIG God who had delivered them. They forgot about this God who parted the Red Sea and allowed them to walk across on dry ground as the Egyptian army was chasing them down. They forgot about that God. As they moved into the Promised Land, over time they began to mix their faith with the ways and practices of other nations they encountered along the way. That's a scary place to be for any believer. There's only one true God. There's only one true Deliverer. There's only one BIG God who can deliver you out of every mess that you've ever gotten into, and who gives you access into heaven. All of this is found in Jesus.

He's a BIG God, and you can't mix what the world has to say with what the Word of God has to say. We need to place our faith completely in what the Word of God has to say. The flip side is that you can become very anxious about your future if you don't focus your attention and faith on God.

As a nation, Israel lost their focus and forgot about the BIG God who had delivered them. Judges 6:1-5 says:

> *The people of Israel did what was evil in the sight*

of the Lord. And the Lord gave them into the hand of Midian seven years, and the hand of Midian prevailed over Israel. And because of Midian the people made for themselves the dens which are in the mountains, and the caves and the strongholds. For whenever the Israelites put in seed into the ground, the Midianites, and the Amalekites, and the people of the East would come and attack them. They would encamp against them and destroy the produce of the land for as far as the neighborhood of Gaza, and leave no sustenance in Israel, and no sheep, or ox, or ass. For they would come up with their cattle and their tents, coming like locusts for the number, both they and their camels would not be counted, so that they wasted the land as they came in.

Prior to entering the Promised Land, the children of Israel had wandered around in the desert for forty years. Now the next generation entered this land that their parents had been telling them about. God had preserved them and finally led them into the land. But even in the Promised Land, there were still problems they had to overcome.

Still an Enemy to Resist

It reminds me of believers who comes to Christ, and think that once they become a believer everything's going to be perfect from that point on. But when they get a cold, hard slap of reality in the face, they quickly turn away from their faith when they find out that there's still an enemy to resist. Too often, that's what happens to people. They come into a relationship of faith in Christ, and they think they're never going to have another problem or attack. They think that everything's going to be perfect. It's true that God will help you live victorious in life. But you're still going to have obstacles that you will have to take to Him.

The Midianites were major obstacles to the children of Israel. They watched and waited while the children of Israel planted their crops. All year long they left God's people alone. But when it was time to harvest the crops, they swept down, trampled the crops, and took whatever they wanted. They took donkeys and sheep and anything else that delighted their eyes. Does this sound like a land you would want promised to you? This isn't the kind of place in which you would want to have a family and raise children.

How It Started

But notice how this first started. Do you remember what Judges 6:1 says? "The people of Israel did what was evil in the sight of the Lord." That was the beginning of their downfall. God had given them the outline and plan to go in and take and maintain the land. One of the first things He said to them was "Do not serve any other gods but Me." But when they entered into the Promised Land, they began to take other faiths and mix them together with theirs. They took on the likeness of the world.

The Bible says do not be conformed to the image of this world, but be transformed by the renewing of your mind (Romans 12:2). In the church today, what we find is that too many believers want to live with one foot in the world and one foot in the church. They try to balance between the two, inevitably trampling on God's grace.

Why does this happen? It seems like there are times when we think God's grace is mainly there to smooth things over for us. There's a tendency to stray from His ways and then we expect God to wink at us with a nod of approval while we carry on a life of sin outside His plan.

But isn't God BIG enough to empower us to live completely and totally for Him? Isn't He BIG enough to help us to live in that holiness that we came into when we first gave our lives to Jesus? For many of us, when we first gave our hearts to Him, we had this compelling sense of love from God and toward God. We knew that something had happened within and Jesus had made us clean. We knew Jesus had made us right and had freed us of all of our wrongs and unrighteousness. Many of us stood with tears in our eyes, and we knew, that we knew, that we knew, that we were forgiven and had a new beginning in life.

But because Israel turned their back on the God that delivered them and made things right, their troubles didn't end once they got into the Promised Land. The Midianites would wait for the harvest, and at the most opportune time they'd strike and take everything Israel had worked for in the fields.

All that hard work was for nothing. People starved. The economy was crumbling. Families were devastated. And there was nothing Israel could do to retaliate. It had been this way for many years and the future looked bleak—it looked like nothing was ever going to change.

You ever felt that way? You work hard week after week. Maybe you go in early, stay late, and maybe you do it for years. Just when it seems that there's a light at the end of the tunnel, maybe you're in line for promotion, and you get called into a meeting where instead of being moved ahead you're let go.

Some people have worked in a place for ten or twenty years and then one day they don't have a job anymore. They were caught in the "downsizing" of the company. The organization's priorities and vision changed. You no longer fit the ideal position they needed filled. Hearing and experiencing that kind of thing will take the wind out of your sails and can fill you with discouragement, frustration, and hopelessness. When it seems you take one step forward and two steps back, it can make you think there's no reason to try doing anything great for the future. That is exactly what Israel felt like. Maybe you've felt this way in the past, or that's how you feel right now.

If it is, what I want you to understand is that God will never leave you. He'll never forsake you. He's bigger than your employer. He's bigger than your finances. God's bigger than everything that you can possibly imagine. We serve a BIG God who will never leave us. He will come through for us. The same BIG God who came to Israel's rescue and raised up a man named Gideon to bring change – that same God will also open up your way of escape from whatever's got you boxed in and held back.

God is BIG for those people who put their faith in Him, and keep it there. Faith in Christ will never fail you. The world will try to sell you a false bill of goods. What you have to determine in your mind and heart is that there is a way that seems right to men who don't know God, but the end of those ways is only going to lead further away from the best that God has planned for their future. The counsel of unbelievers is all smoke and mirrors trying to lure you from a good and hopeful future. You have to determine that you want the real deal for your future. The real deal comes from knowing with certainty, and living out with confidence, what God says about your future.

One key thing we must understand is that God is going to go BIG in the future of those people who put their faith in Him. When you put your faith in how BIG God is, you don't have to worry about your future. Let's consider a few things that will help you to have faith for your future.

Run to Him

If you're in a tight position and you're wondering how BIG God is, you have to run to Him. If you've turned your back on God, or put your faith in things that the world has suggested will help, it's time to reprioritize! To change your future, realize your first cry for help should be to God. Judges 6:6, says, "Midian…so impoverished the Israelites that they cried out to the Lord for help."

Why did they cry out to the Lord for help? They sought God because they were impoverished and oppressed under a system of lack. Things had gotten so bad that poverty covered the land. But the worst part of the story is that poverty invaded the minds and hearts of the people. It saturated their thinking and affected their relationships. When financial stress attacks a family, the stress of poverty and lack turns people into something other than what they want to be. When lack is an everyday thing, people can have short fuses, and frustration and anger alters personalities. Where joy and laughter once prevailed, it's replaced by fear for the future.

In times of distress, people may flock to churches looking for comfort and answers. When things get bad enough, some people do run to Jesus, and that's great! If it takes a little bit of hardship for people to flood into church and it stirs a revival, then at least we're seeing people repent and come to church to find God. I want to see people cry out for a God who's BIG in their lives. The Israelites cried out for God to do something big in their lives, families, homes, and nation. They wanted a better future for themselves, and for their children.

In the midst of all their troubles, they believed that a BIG God that delivered them out of the hands of the Egyptians could also deliver them now from the Midianites.

Do you remember the things that God has done for you in your life? Think back to the times when God came through for you. Think about times when you were not sure if God was really going to come through, when it seemed there was no way out, but somehow He made a way when there seemed to be no way. If He was BIG enough to do it then, He's BIG enough to do it now.

Psalm 86:5 says: "For thou, O Lord, art good and forgiving, abounding in steadfast love to all who call on thee." God is no respecter of persons. He promised that all who call on him are positioned to receive the benefits of His goodness, His forgiveness, and His steadfast love. As Israel cried out to the Lord, He responded by sending a prophet to them who said through the Spirit of God, "I led you out of Egypt. I delivered you out of slavery and out of the hand of your oppressors. I gave you this land, but you didn't listen when I told you do not worship anything other than me."

In His mercy and love, God sent the answer to their problems through the words of this prophet. Sometimes our answers come in the form of correction for re-direction. Many times God will remind us of things He's told or shown us before. In this case, God told them they had strayed from Him and worshipped other gods. When they cried out, God told them what to do to change their future.

If we're not careful, the love and faith we have for God, or once had for Him, can begin to wane just like Israel's did. We can forget how faithful and mighty God has been and is to us. We can lose sight of just how big God is and we can try to look for answers in other places and do things on our own. We are so much better off when we put our faith in Christ and let Him help us through these times. These may be hard times for you right now. Where you stand in your life today, you may feel depressed about your future. These may be times that you don't know if you can make it through this on your own. You're probably right. On your own, you most likely won't be able to make it successfully through.

But by placing your faith in God and crying out to Him, He'll help you. He'll be there for you. Just like He has always done in the past, He'll be a BIG God for you now. Just like He helped Israel in the midst of very troublesome times, He'll help you out of your troubles. The scriptures say that God never changes and Jesus Himself is the same yesterday, today and forever. You can rely on Him when you cry out to Him.

If God would go BIG in Bible days, He will go BIG for you today. When is the last time you believed God for something big in your life? When's the last time you just said, "God, this is what your Word says, I'm just going to believe you for it. God, You said if I started paying my tithe that you would rebuke the devourer. You said if I seek you first, and your kingdom, and your righteousness, you would add everything I need in life. Lord, I'm going to stand on your Word for that."

I know it can be hard to stand, speak, and believe those things sometimes. And when you get out into the world and go about living your daily life, things can beat you up a little bit. But if you'll keep your faith in Him, if you'll cry out to God, He'll move BIG in your future. Too many times I've seen people graduate from high school or college, or get married and start raising a family, and get immersed in their jobs and get distracted. I've watched as people moved God's Word, the church, and even fellowship with other believers, way down on their list of priorities. Before long, life starts to tear apart the fabric of everything for which they have worked. It's not long before their circumstances get them to wondering what happened to the victory they used to have in their lives.

The answer always begins with coming back and

crying out to God. That's what this prophet told Israel. But when you cry out to God, be prepared to humble yourself before God. When you cry out to a BIG God He asks you to repent and change some things that have taken hold in your life. That's what had to happen for Israel to be free from the oppression of their enemies.

Repent

The second thing to understand is they had to repent. Literally, the word repent means "to change." There had to come a change of perspective and change of mind and heart. Israel had to see God for who He was and who He was to be, not only in their lives and families, but also in the nation. Accompanied by a change of mind and heart, God will always give directions for a change in behavior. Sometimes the changes can be simple details and new habits. Other times, the changes God requires are broad brushstrokes to usher in a new way of doing life His way. In either event, God promises that He will radically transform the lives of the ones who change their hearts, minds, and behaviors. And God will never go back on His promises.

In II Chronicles 7:14, God promised that, "If My people, who are called by my name, will humble themselves, pray and seek My face, and turn from their wicked ways, then I will hear from heaven and I will forgive their sin, and heal their land." God had a plan for the Israelites, but they weren't following it. Anytime that you get off from the plan of God and start to do things in your own power, your own will, in your own way, that's when the enemies come and try to steal everything for which you've worked so hard.

The good and hopeful news is that turning your full attention back to God, with humility, causes you to see things clearly once again. When you decide to pursue God daily with a transparency and determination to walk closely with Him through thick and thin, this invites the biggest promises of God to come true in your life.

I look around the world and see that God needs believers, churches, young people just out of high school or college, seasoned professionals, and faithful families to be the generation that will stand up and trust Him to be BIG in their lives. I'm praying for a generation—the current generation and the older generation together in unity—to rise up and return back to God in full force. We need God to move in our culture and society. We need real revival in our communities and homes. I hunger for us to see the God who works miracles, signs, and wonders in the earth. I'm seeking for the bigger promises of

God to come true for you and me. But none of this happens without living in step with II Chronicles 7:14. And this scripture requires a repentant, easy to work with, and easy to shape, heart. This heart attitude creates an atmosphere that invites a move of God.

You can tell when a move of God comes. The way we know big things are in the works is because people start repenting—changing on purpose to align their lives with the Word and ways of God. People catch themselves being convicted of things that they've done for years and thought to be ok, but now they start to change. God will make you aware of habits that need to change and ask you to repent. This is one of the signposts on the road to personal revival. When that spirit of change sweeps through a group of believers, that's when revival begins to affect a family, a community, even a nation!

In Judges 6, God came to Gideon to initiate the change for which Israel was crying out. In the middle of the night, Gideon was threshing wheat in a winepress. He was hiding in fear from the Midianites. He didn't want them to know that he was threshing wheat. He wanted to hide his harvest from them. He was afraid they would come down like in times past and take everything for which he had diligently labored. In the midst of what was supposed to be the Israelites dream land, here was Gideon hiding and threshing wheat in the cover of darkness.

This was the land where the table was always to be full, where there was to be a chariot in every garage, a land of plenty and more than enough. Everything was supposed to be wonderful. But you remember how chapter 6 started. Judges 6:1—But the people did evil in the sight of the Lord. They did *evil* in the sight of the Lord, even though they were in the Promised Land.

Think about this picture. If Gideon had any insight about Israel's history, he knew they had a covenant that promised blessing, yet he's under a curse. He would have known they were supposed to be the head and not the tail, above and not beneath. While he's threshing wheat on this particular night, he might have been grumbling and complaining and considering how far away he was at that moment from what God promised. He was not openly blessed. He was hiding to preserve what little bit of harvest he had.

Lost in his thoughts, as he was hiding and threshing the wheat, God appeared to Gideon. Judges 6:12 says, "And the angel of the Lord appeared to him and said, the Lord is with you, mighty man of valor." Imagine the Lord appearing and speaking to you while you're complaining against Him. Despite Gideon's frustrations, fears, and hopelessness, God said He was with him and called Gideon *a mighty man of valor*. Gideon's response is fairly typical.

"And Gideon said to him, I pray, sir, if the Lord is with us, then why then has all this befallen us. And where are all the wonderful deeds our fathers recounted to us, saying, did not the Lord bring us up out of Egypt."

To summarize, he said, "If you're with me and I'm such a mighty man of valor, why has all this happened to me and to our people, and why am I hiding in hopes of having enough food to survive another season? Why are we always struggling to make it?"

God's words are very revealing. God is always looking at a problem from the vantage point of the winner. He sees the successful result already accomplished. His views are always from the standard of truth and reality. God's view of things IS the way things truly are. We might be hiding from the enemy, but what God says is, "No, I've made you an overcomer and more than a conqueror." God sees the results He can create when people believe His Word.

Ultimately Gideon realized that God was speaking to him. And notice how God regards and speaks to this man.

God saw a good and hopeful future and He called him as He saw him, in this future. Romans 4:17 says, "He is the God who calls into existence the things that do not exist." The world sees the Gideons of the world as weak, incapable of greatness, impoverished with no hope of things changing. God calls these very same Gideons *mighty men and women of valor*. You are what *God* calls you, not what others call you.

If God calls you blessed, you're blessed. If God calls you healed, you're healed. If God calls you favored, you're favored. If God calls you a mighty man or woman of valor, regardless of what it looks or feels like, that's exactly what you are. When God says, "man or woman of God, you're going to raise up finances and pour wealth and strength into the kingdom of God," then you hold onto that dream because that's exactly what's going to happen. Even when men may predict that the end is coming and all hope is lost, cling to the promised Word of God. People may try to speak negative things into your life, but the word of God trumps the words of men. Listen to what God says and you'll succeed in living the life of His dreams for you.

Stop Settling

If you are going to see God move BIG in your future, then you can't settle for the status quo. We can't settle for doing church as normal. It's a time to see your family members saved. It's a time to see your community saved and aflame with godly fires of revival and reformation. We will not settle for how we've done church in the past because God is calling the twenty-first century church to be the place where dynamic, radical and lasting transformations happen in the lives of those who step through our doors.

Just like we saw in Acts, we win the lost and see multitudes come to God in the fear of the Lord. We are under the Lordship of Jesus, the Head of the church, and we affect not only our communities, and our nation, but also all the nations of the earth. We have multi-generational thinkers who rise up and believe God that He's just as BIG as He's always been and He's just as big as He says He is.

I believe we are poised and on the verge of some of the greatest moves of God our generation has ever seen. But we can't settle for the miracles and reports from the past. Just as Gideon was saying the miracles of our forefathers were in the past, these examples are to encourage us to experience our own in the present. This is our time to take up the mantle of revival for the purpose of fulfilling all God's good will in our generation.

This isn't the time to settle for status quo, but rather the time to pray and be a willing vessel for the Master's use. It's time to say, "God, I crucify my flesh before you, so that if I see a sick person today, I know that the Holy Spirit is in me, that I may lay hands on the sick and see them recover." God is looking for the men and women, the teenagers and children who will rise up and just believe Him like Gideon came to believe Him.

If we want to see God go BIG in our lives, we cannot settle for "business as usual." How can we expect to have something different and better by doing the outdated things that never have produced the results we desire? Gideon could have kept threshing wheat in the darkness of the winepress and Israel's circumstances would have been no different, no better. But because Gideon determined to believe God and act on what He told him to do, things changed.

Gideon chose to resist settling for stolen harvest to be the story of his life. Just like Gideon didn't settle as a captive to an embittered and fruitless life, don't you settle for things that are less than God's best! If God's Word promises more than you're experiencing, then it's up to you to believe God's Word until you see what He says He's provided for you. Don't settle for less than His best for you.

Believe What He Says About You

If you're not going to settle for less than God's best, you have to believe what He says to you and about you. Believing God requires you to resist the urge to make excuses about why God's promises to you aren't taking place. In Judges 6:14, God said, "Go, in this might of yours…" Immediately, Gideon started making excuses. "But Lord, how can I save Israel? My clan is the weakest and I'm the least in all my family." Gideon was saying, "I'm nothing, I'm nobody, I'm uneducated and I'm puny."

You may think that because you were not raised in church, or you didn't finish school, or you've made mistakes, or you cussed out your family, and kicked your dog, that you're disqualified from serving God and doing great things for Him. Remember what we said earlier: Repent—change your mind, heart, and behavior.

The forgiveness and mercy of God is new every morning, and He's faithful to restore you to the path He's always had for you. You can only use sin as an excuse if you decide not to repent and decide to continue in sin. But why would you want to do that? God will help you overcome sin and to cast off the weights that seek to hold you back. God's with you,

He's helping you and He calls you mighty.

Even if you're going through hard times, God hasn't changed His mind about you. Trust Him. He's a BIG God. He can handle whatever obstacles that stand in your way. No more excuses. You can do all things through Christ, and through Him you'll do more than you ever dreamed or imagined. You'll be more than an overcomer. Trust God and He'll direct your steps and make your path smooth and straight. If you're in Christ, you're a new creation. God isn't condemning you. He's the One giving you a lift and helping hand through life so that you mount up with wings as eagles and soar through life. God has great plans for you.

Take to heart the words of Jeremiah 29:11 where God said, "I know the plans that I have for you, declares the Lord, plans to prosper you and not to harm you, plans to give you hope and a future." God was saying, "I'm going to be BIG in your future if you'll just put your trust in Me. You won't be on your own."

And isn't that exactly what happened as Gideon put His trust in God and relied upon Him? As God spoke to him, a tide of confidence began to rise up within Gideon. But also a sense of purpose grew within him. The spiritual dissatisfaction he felt from the whole country turning away from God rose up within him as well and he believed that God could use him to do great exploits in the earth. God saw the greatness in Gideon, drew it out of him, and Gideon became that mighty man of valor who was instrumental in leading Israel to overcome the enemy that had oppressed his people for so many years. Gideon believed in how BIG God was and as a result, God became BIG in creating a greater future for Gideon, his family and his nation.

Some years back there was a practice session going badly for the Green Bay Packers. More specifically, it was going bad for one of their offensive lineman. He was missing blocks, forgetting plays, jumping off sides and generally making all kinds of mistakes. His coach, the legendary Vince Lombardi, finally told the player that he was finished for the day and to hit the locker room.

An hour or so later as Lombardi was passing through the locker room, there sat the man. Discouraged, this lineman was still in his pads and sobbing like a little boy. Seeing this, Coach Lombardi walked over to the man and with the compassion of a father put his arm around him. The coach remarked, "I meant what I said today about you playing terrible. But what I need to tell you is the rest of the story. You see, inside of you is a great football player, and I'm going to help you find him and bring him out."

That player, Jerry Kramer, went on to be a 5-time all-pro lineman at only 6'3" and 250 lbs. A few years ago he was even named the all-time best offensive guard to play in the first 50 years of football. Vince Lombardi had the insightful capacity to see greatness in his players' abilities that they didn't themselves know they had. He believed they all had great futures, if they would just realize the greatness they had within.

God believes in you the same way. At God's directions, Gideon selected 300 men to fight alongside him. Then this man, who was from the puniest clan, and who had once hid out in a winepress, led these 300 men to tackle insurmountable odds. God saw the greatness within Gideon, and Gideon trusted God to be BIG in his future. They defeated the enemy because they believed that God was with them.

In the very same way, God is looking for men and women, young people, leaders, and churches who will cry out to Him and repent where necessary. God is looking for the ones who won't settle for the status quo and will believe what He says about them. God is looking for people who will rely on Him to be BIG in their future. Are you one of them? If so, God has BIG plans for you!

Chapter Eight: Allowing God to Be Big Through Yo

Dangers of Complacency

As I have traveled the world to minister in many different settings, I have noticed some commonalities in the global church. It seems that regardless of geography, many Christians settle into a place of dangerous comfort in their faith. Don't get me wrong here – being *confident* in your faith is a good thing, but being *comfortable* is quite another. The Word of God warns us in 1 Corinthians 10:12, "Therefore let him who thinks he stands take heed lest he fall." This BIG God that we've been talking about wants you to know His power that is available to you, but He does not want you becoming so comfortable that complacence settles in. Complacence can cause you to let your guard down against your enemy, and soon you could be distracted from what God's purpose is for your life and the lives of those around you.

It's easy to be distracted isn't it? We live in an A.D.D. world that's filled with many things that can cause us to go from endeavor to endeavor while never really focusing on what's important.

I recently read a story of two great baseball players. It involved Yogi Berra, the well-known catcher for the New York Yankees, and Hank Aaron, who at that time was the chief power hitter for the Milwaukee Braves. The teams were playing in the World Series, and as usual Yogi was keeping up his ceaseless chatter, intended to pep up his teammates on the one hand, and distract the Milwaukee batters on the other. As Aaron came to the plate, Yogi tried to distract him by saying, "Henry, you're holding the bat wrong. You're supposed to hold it so you can read the trademark."

Aaron didn't say anything, but when the next pitch came he hit it into the left-field bleachers. After rounding the bases and tagging up at home plate, Aaron looked at Yogi Berra and said, "I didn't come up here to read."

Sadly, I see this often in both churches and individual Christians. Churches get distracted from what their mission really is. Have you ever stopped to consider, "What is the mission of the church and what exactly is your role in it?"

- *Does the church only exist to provide a place of worship for you and your family?*

- *Is it there to make sure our deceased loved ones are memorialized properly?*

- *Does the church exist so we can have a great place to host our weddings?*

- *Or, maybe the church exists to provide a place for us to make friends?*

While these are all wonderful reasons to belong to a local church, they are not the reason for the existence of the church.

In fact, such inward thinking is what leads Christians and churches alike, to be distracted from God's original mission for them. Unfortunately, you can always know when it starts to happen too. Arguments begin to arise about trivial things that are only temporary. How the seating is arranged, colored lighting, styles of worship music, and the Pastor wearing jeans on Sunday mornings, are all things that do not have significance in the light of eternity, yet many are inwardly focused on such things.

Individual believers are not innocent from such thinking either. Inward thinking causes men to be distracted by the allure of making more money or living in a larger home. Inward thinking causes women to compare themselves to those that have more than they do. Inward thinking causes our children to think that life is all about the here and now. Distractions come to us all, but isn't our faith and our relationship with God so much bigger than the here and now? So, what exactly is the mission of the church? What exactly are we to be doing as believers?

What is Our Mission?

I believe that Jesus was giving us the answer to such questions when He allowed a glimpse of His early childhood to be recorded in Luke 2:41-49.

> *His parents went to Jerusalem every year at the Feast of the Passover. And when He was twelve years old, they went up to Jerusalem according to the custom of the feast. When they had finished the days, as they returned, the Boy Jesus lingered behind in Jerusalem. And Joseph and His mother did not know it; but supposing Him to have been in the company, they went a day's journey, and sought Him among their relatives and acquaintances. So when they did not find Him, they*

returned to Jerusalem, seeking Him. Now so it was that after three days they found Him in the temple, sitting in the midst of the teachers, both listening to them and asking them questions. And all who heard Him were astonished at His understanding and answers. So when they saw Him, they were amazed; and His mother said to Him, "Son, why have You done this to us? Look, Your father and I have sought You anxiously." And He said to them, "Why did you seek Me? Did you not know that I must be about My Father's business?" But they did not understand the statement which He spoke to them.

Can you imagine being Joseph and Mary at that moment? One minute you're laughing and chatting it up with your family on the long ride home, and the next you realize that you have LOST THE SON OF GOD! How would they explain that to God?

"Um…well, God it was very busy when we started to leave the city and I was trying to pack the wagon quickly to beat the morning traffic."

I can't help but laugh just a little at the thought of the moment when they realized that Jesus had been left.

Mary says to her husband, "Joseph, where's Jesus?"

Joseph answers, "What do you mean 'where's Jesus?' I thought he was with you. "

This leads us to a sobering question, *How distracted do you have to be to leave Jesus behind?* Yet, believers and churches do it all the time.

In order for us to protect ourselves from being so distracted that we leave Jesus behind, we must do what Jesus was doing at the time. Look again to what Jesus said: "I must be about my Father's business."

If Jesus had to be about the Father's business and recorded the fact for us in scripture, doesn't it stand to reason that He would want us to be about the Father's business as well? Have you ever stopped to wonder why this is the only recorded history we have of Jesus' early childhood? God was showing us that even in the midst of the busyness of life, we are to be about the Father's business. We must not allow ourselves to be distracted by inward thinking, busyness, jobs, or any other thing that should try to rob us of God's true mission in this world.

What Exactly Is The Father's Business?

As we dive deeper into this, we find that God has given us

very specific examples of what exactly His business is. Take a look at John 8 for example. We find a story of a woman who was caught in the act of adultery. The Bible is clear that she was "in the very act" of adultery when she was apprehended. The religious people took her to Jesus and threw her at His feet. While she was no doubt hiding her face in shame, the leaders tested Jesus by reminding that the law commanded such a woman to be stoned to death. You can imagine the terrifying experience this woman was going through. Not only was she feeling the guilt of her shame, but also now was being humiliated and threatened with death, publically.

I love how Jesus handles this situation. I wish I could tell you that I would have acted in the same manner as our Savior. I wish that I could tell you that most church members would have followed His example if there. Unfortunately, I can't. Our loving Savior pretends not to hear the religious leaders at all. He simply stoops down and begins to write in the dirt with his finger. After a few moments of silence, Jesus stands once again and says, "He who is without sin among you, let him throw a stone at her first" (John 8:7).

The story goes on to record how each of the accusers dropped their stones one by one and walked away. After they were all gone, Jesus leans down to the women that still lay at his feet and asks, "Women, where are your accusers?"

She replies, "There are none."

Then we see a wonderful example of who Jesus really is, when He responds, and "Neither do I condemn you, go and sin no more."

Why wouldn't Jesus be angry at such a women? Why wouldn't He just make an example of her? In my way of thinking it would seem that this was a perfect opportunity to show all of those who want to commit adultery, the consequences of their sin. If we were honest, you and I would probably have been just as angry as the religious leaders.

What if that had been your spouse caught in the very act of adultery? While we would like to think we would act as graciously as Jesus, the truth is, most of us would not. I believe we wouldn't because we forget that this woman is a representation of what we have done to Christ ourselves. We forget that we too, have been caught cheating on God many times. We too were not deserving of the mercy of Jesus. Fortunately for us, and for the woman in this story, God doesn't think like we do. He is a merciful God Who loves His children and wants them to know His grace.

Why is this story in the Bible? To show us how Jesus was being about the Father's business and the Father's business is about saving lost souls! Shouldn't our business be the same?

God's Heart

I would submit to you that the heart of God is to save lost people. In fact, I would be so bold to say that if God could give you one thing and nothing more, it would be your salvation. He longs so dearly to be in a relationship with you that He would do anything to have it. Even allow the death of His Son on a cross. While, it isn't the only thing that God has given to man, it is the most important. God's heart is for the salvation of all mankind. The Bible tells us that He isn't willing that any should perish, but that all should come to repentance. The woman caught in adultery is no different than you and me in that we need the salvation that only Jesus can provide. Make no mistake about it. The Father's business is salvation, and ours should be the same.

When was the last time you intentionally shared your faith with someone? Last week? Last month? Last year? Ever? I know that's a challenging set of questions and can be a little scary, but have you considered the consequences of remaining quiet with such news? We must break free from the distractions of this life and begin to peer into the consequences of eternity! The lives of people are hanging in the balance of a simple message that will change their eternal destinies! You are empowered by the Holy Spirit to be about the Father's business of salvation. His heart has been revealed to you, now is the time to reveal His heart to others.

God's Hand

In Matthew 14 Jesus feeds 5000 hungry people. In John 11 He raises Lazarus from the dead. In countless other places in scripture we see the hand of God reaching out to those who are in physical need. What was Jesus doing when feeding people, healing people, showing compassion toward people? He was being about the Father's business! If salvation is the *heart* of God, then compassion is the *hand* of God. Unfortunately, many believers today have become so distracted with the concerns of this life, that they are either unwilling or unaware of the pains of others around them.

Many years ago, when my son was just a small boy, we were traveling through a large city. I had been discussing with my wife in the front seat about ministering to some homeless men the night before. As I spoke with her about the evening before, my son spoke from the back seat asking where the homeless people slept if they did not have houses. I began to explain to him that they slept wherever they could find shelter and that many times it's under bridges and overpasses. There was a long pause from the back seat and I could see my son looking under each overpass that we encountered.

Finally, he said to me, "Daddy why haven't I ever seen them before?"

I in turn asked him, "Why do you think you've never seen them, Buddy?"

Again, there was a long pause. His reply? "I guess I haven't ever looked for them."

When is the last time that you have looked for someone to help? Are you just driving through life never slowing down to look for the hurting around you? My friend, you and I must slow down and be the hand of God in the lives of other people. I want to challenge you to begin today by looking for those around you who are in need.

We are called to be about the Fathers business and that business is being the hand of God. When you reach out and provide for the physical need of someone else, you're going about the Fathers business. The single parent who is struggling, the elderly in your neighborhood, the homeless, and countless millions in undeveloped countries are in need of the hand of God in their lives. Who will reach out to them if we do not? Many are so burdened with the stresses of this life that only an act of kindness will open their hearts to the Gospel message. Your small act of kindness could be the very reason someone surrenders his or her life to Jesus.

The Word of God

The heart of God is salvation and the hand of God is compassion, but the Word of God is education. God wants us to be involved in His business of bringing people to Him, showing compassion to them and then teaching them about His promises. Consider our example of Luke 2 again. Where was Jesus and what was He doing? The Bible says He was in the temple and all who were there were amazed by his understanding and answers. Obviously, Jesus was reasoning, teaching, and learning with the religious leaders of the day. He was educated in the things of God and not just because He was Jesus. That passage goes on to say that Jesus grew in wisdom and stature. Did you catch that? Jesus *grew* in wisdom. Does that astound you like it does me? Jesus – the Savior of the world; God in the flesh – grew in wisdom.

Apparently, Jesus thought that being in the temple and reasoning out the things of God was beneficial. It is pretty clear to me that God is showing us that growing in our faith does not come automatically. Especially if Jesus had to grow! So what does that mean for you and me? Of course it means that being about the Father's business carries an element of growing in wisdom, but also helping others grow in theirs.

According to Matthew 28, we are called to go to all the nations of the world and make disciples. Jesus is clear that He's not looking to make converts, but rather followers. Many times in the New Testament people did not understand Jesus because He was not giving them a set of rules to follow, instead He was teaching them Who God was. This is an important concept to understand for us today. Jesus is not calling us to teach the Word of God to people so they can recite the books of the Bible. Nor is His ultimate goal to see people memorize long passages of scripture. Are these things important? Sure they are, but not for why some might think.

Jesus commands us to go and make disciples because He knows the closer they get to His Word, the closer they are getting to a relationship with Him. Educating people in the Word of God helps them to fall in love with Jesus, but secondly to understand who they are in Him!

Do you see how liberating this can be for someone who does not know who God is or what is available to them? When you know who you are, no one can convince you otherwise! Helping others know who they are in Christ is at the heart of discipleship. When Jesus calls us to go and make disciples, He is asking us to help people understand who He is, who they are, and what is available to them!

Throughout this book so far we've discussed what God has done and what's available to us. I am now shifting that focus to help you understand that God has not brought you this far simply so you could live in victory all by yourself. Not at all. He's taught you that He's bigger than your past, your sickness, and your problems, so that you can go and testify of that fact to others!

You may be thinking, "But, Jerod I don't know how to teach the Bible."

I'm not asking you to go and teach the Bible, I'm simply asking you to go and tell your story. Your God story. Tell others about what He's done in your life. What has he saved you from? What has He healed you from? What is He doing in your life right now? Telling your own God story helps others to have faith of their own.

Why This Matters

It's imperative that you understand at this point what I'm trying to communicate. In order for God to be big in your life, you must make him big to others. It's of paramount importance that your faith makes a shift from thinking inwardly about your own spiritual growth, to thinking outwardly of the lost and hurting of this world. In fact, I would submit to you that you haven't fully come to a mature place in your faith until it becomes outward. We can no longer sit idly by as this world consumes the lives of those around us. We must act, and it must be now. If we don't, it *will matter*.

It will matter as it did in 1994 in the tiny country of Rwanda. Ethnic tensions had built for years between the Hutu and Tutsi tribes and when the president of Rwanda had his plane shot down, the Hutu took an opportunity to exterminate the Tutsi once and for all.

Armed with machetes, rebel Hutu groups swept through the country murdering innocent Tutsi families at the rate of 8,000 a day. As the horror continued for weeks and the body count became impossible to comprehend, the international community did nothing.

Tutsis were calling out to the international community for assistance only to fall on deaf ears. Even here in the US, we were debating in Washington over the definition of genocide instead of sending help. One hundred days later over 800,000 people in Rwanda were dead. How could an atrocity like this take place? It could only happen when those who *can* do something, choose not to. What we do with the message of Jesus matters.

It matters to the little boy I met in Hosanna, Ethiopia. We were there conducting a large crusade in the village. Night after night we watched as over 275,000 people gathered to hear the Gospel of Jesus. Literally thousands gave their lives to Christ over that four days, but what impacted me the most was the encounter I had with this little boy in the village.

During one of the days of ministry, we went to a small mud church to feed the orphan children of the village. When I walked into the church I could smell the food which had began to pile up, plate by plate on the small platform behind the pulpit. After recognizing the smell of food, I looked to the back of the room and saw a man standing in front of a door made from bamboo and twine. He was holding the door shut, but just beyond him I could see small little faces peering at me through the cracks in the door.

Once the door was opened, a rush of children of all sizes came in and sat down on the small wooden benches of the church. I was immediately overwhelmed by the condition of these children. Dirty, rags for clothes, and suffering from malnutrition, doesn't even begin to relate what I saw that day. As they sat somewhat patiently waiting for food, the leaders asked me to tell a Bible story while they finished preparing the food.

As I told them about the Apostle Paul, I could barely get through the story without tears. God was arresting my heart like never before. They watched intently as I spoke about the life of Paul. Their faces seemed to be mesmerized by the white man who was speaking through an interpreter. As I acted out a story from Paul's life I could tell that they were more interested in the food behind me than they were the Bible story, so I quickly finished.

Soon, it was time to pass out the food. As I stood passing out plates to these small children, I couldn't help but wonder where their next meal was coming from; however, I felt good that they were able to eat today. One by one they passed by, took their plate, and found a place in the church to eat.

Just as we were almost out of plates, one little boy came into the back of the church. He stood all by himself, not knowing what to do. He was trembling uncontrollably and covered with layers of dirty clothing. I quickly noticed that he was losing his hair from malnutrition and his hands were swollen, with one lame and tucked to his side. As he approached slowly toward the stage where we were passing out the food, I noticed that his feet were swollen and dry, and caked with dirt. The sides of his little feet had been cracked open and bleeding recently from the neglect. His eyes looked up to make contact with mine, just as I handed him the plate of food.

He took the plate and tucked his lame hand under it for support. Sitting down quickly, he began to shovel the food into his mouth like he hadn't eaten in days. I couldn't believe what I was seeing. How could this be possible in our world? How could there still be places on this planet where little boys and girls were going hungry? The longer I watched the madder I got at God. Soon, I could take no more and I left the church and found a place to weep.

For the next two days, I could barely sleep or eat. The images of this boy were somehow lodged in my head, not to be removed. My anger at God was growing as I pondered how He could sit idly by as children starved to death in the world He created. Finally, it was time to board the plane and return to America, but on the flight I could not shake this feeling that I was forever changed by the experience of one little boy.

Not being able to eat or sleep on the flight, I began to write in my journal. Onto its pages I spilled my anger at God. I was honest with Him in that I did not understand why He would let this happen. It just did not make sense to me that a God who saved me would in turn allow such atrocity to exist. Emotions overcame me and I began to cry uncontrollably. I quickly closed my journal and buried my face into my hands, weeping for several minutes. "Why God?" I thought in my mind over and over. "How can you allow this to happen and why don't you do something?" These questions haunted me for several minutes as others on the plane no doubt thought I was having some sort of episode.

Then, in a gentle and loving way, God began to speak to my heart. I felt Him say, "You ask me why I would allow this to happen and why I don't do something; but I guess I could ask you the same question."

Suddenly, I had a revelation like I have never experienced in my life. Here I was mad at God for not doing something about the poverty in the world, and He was asking me the same question. It was at that moment, that I realized how ridiculous it was for me to blame God for the hungry of the world, when clearly there was enough food to go around for the entire world. I realized at that moment, that God doesn't have a shortage of people to help, but rather a shortage of people who are *willing* to help.

I picked up my pen and wrote in my journal that day,

"God if no one will go, I will go. If no one will help, I will help. If no one will speak on their behalf, I will speak."

My friend, God doesn't have a harvest problem, He has a labor problem. This is why He tells us in Luke 10:2 "The harvest is plentiful, but the laborers are few" (NIV). We must take this big God and share him with the world. We can make a difference with the Gospel of Jesus by displaying the heart of God, the hand of God and the Word of God to the hurting and hungry of this world. Make no mistake, God truly becomes big in our lives, when we are focused on making Him big in the lives of others.

My Final Challenge

My challenge to you is to find something God is doing that's bigger than yourself and get involved. Take a mission trip, financially support a missionary, volunteer at the local homeless shelter, or get involved with your local church. People need you and God needs you. Begin today by stepping out of the norm and doing something big for God. It's time for you to start living bigger than you've ever imagined.

To learn more about the ministry of Jerod Smith,
please visit: www.advocatesforafrica.org

Made in the USA
Charleston, SC
11 June 2016